MALADIES

A NOVEL BY
VIRGINIA NIELSEN

KITSAP PUBLISHING

Maladies
First edition, published 2019

By Virginia Nielsen

Copyright © 2019, Virginia Nielsen

ISBN-13: 978-1-942661-23-8

This is a work of fiction. Names, characters, businesses, places, events and incidents are either the products of the author's imagination or used in a fictitious manner. Any resemblance to actual persons, living or dead, or actual events is purely coincidental.

All rights reserved. No part of this book may be reproduced or transmitted in any form or by any means, electronic or mechanical, including photocopying, recording or by any information storage and retrieval system, without written permission from the author, except for the inclusion of brief quotations in a review.

Published by Kitsap Publishing
P.O. Box 572
Poulsbo, WA 98370
www.KitsapPublishing.com

I would like to dedicate this book series to my daughter Chloe, her loving father, and step siblings. Thank you all for your love and support through our hard times and those to come.

With Love, Virginia Nielsen

Table of Contents

Chapter 1 - WAR	1
Chapter 2 - THE CHANGE	19
Chapter 3 - TRAINING	25
Chapter 4 - IDENTITY	29
Chapter 5 - COMBAT	39
Chapter 6 - NEXT PLEASE	42
Chapter 7 - MAX	47
Chapter 8 - PANTHER	58
Chapter 9 - THE MISSION	67
Chapter 10 - THE PLAN	85
Chapter 11 - RETURNING HOME	90
Chapter 12 - THE DARK ONES	96
Chapter 13 - BEGINNING	100
Chapter 14 - TRAINING	107
Chapter 15 - MALADIES	118
Chapter 16 - HEALING AND PLANNING	122
Chapter 17 - STEP ONE	126
Chapter 18 - THE AFTERMATH	133
Chapter 19 - THE BATTLE BEGINS	136

Chapter 1

WAR

My name is Sam, and I live in a world long lost, destroyed by war, and illness. My story starts in what was once Alaska. We lived in a big house outside Anchorage. My father was a fisherman, and my mother worked at a local hospital as a nurse. We lived as a middle-class family, we did not have much to show for it, but we loved what we had. I had a little brother named TJ, and he was ten when the war started. I, of course, was sixteen, not very popular, but had a few friends, and could not complain. Life in the world during the twentieth century was pretty good.

Then, World War III broke out. Shortly after a plague spread throughout the world, changing my life forever. One day, my brother and I were in school when the warning sirens rang out. I was in English class, and we were talking about the book "How to Kill a Mocking Bird." We were all focused on the discussion when the siren rang out over the speakers; many students jumped and screamed. My whole class started running for the door. It was chaos. Kids were running from each room and asking teachers who in the hall what to do. A few students had been trampled and lay on the floor. I did my best to help those I found and pull them to their feet.

By the time I got outside and headed towards the middle school, the siren was off, and a male voice announced to all students their families would be picking them up shortly from the gym. I ran straight for my brother, TJ was scared, crying, and did not know what to do. I assured him there was nothing to fear, it was just another test "Well, I hoped it was."

It took us about fifteen minutes to run home. I had to stop several times to usher my brother forward. Once we stepped inside our house, my father and mother were both waiting for us anxiously. They knew to try to pick us up, would be nuts, with all the crazy going on outside. TJ and I were very worried, and from what I could see our parents where too. My mom was working at the hospital. When over the news she watched life in the world-changing before her eyes. The US had been invaded, and World War three started. Mom could not believe what she was watching; it was madness. The news reporter was telling the public to go indoors and brace themselves for what is coming.

Meanwhile, dad was working on the boat when he heard the news over the radio. They were, reporting the destruction, and mass killings across the U.S. His first thought was of his family. He began packing our boat with everything he had stored up over the past few months. Dad had been watching the televised NATO reports the last few months. Each report showed an increase in hostility between nations and talks of war. After dad finished loading the boat, he rushed home, where he found my mom crying laying on the floor.

She had no words to describe what she had seen on the news. Once she had explained to dad, the bombs dropped were filled with some kind chemical enhanced virus. He gasped and became more focused on his family and how he might keep them safe. She explained to him that people who did not die in the bombs began changing. They began looking ill, some seemed to be stronger, had different personal facial features, and others turned into something entirely different, monsters.

The monsters were eating people and causing destruction everywhere. Dad then told mom about his plan. He had been saving up food and supplies for months, and all the boat needed now was us. That is when my brother and I walked into the house. We were quickly ushered to the car and the sailboat. On our way to the boat, people were running, driving on sidewalks, smashing into buildings and homes, it was nothing I had seen before. People where so scared and frantic, they lost all humanity for others around them. When we arrived at the boat, I helped dad push off and start the motor. The marina was dead quiet, and an eerie feeling passed over me. All I could hear was the roar of our boat engine.

My mind drifted to my friends and the life I was leaving behind. What was going to happen to my friends and family? How would we survive out here in the open water, the war would last months! What was my dad thinking? He must have known this was coming, or he would not have been this prepared. He had us all be quiet as we drifted out of the marina and into the open water. He thought others might be watching. They might try and escape on our boat and take it from us.

Days later, in the middle of know where I might add, my father turned on the radio, he wanted to see what might be happening in the world around us, since our voyage began. From what I could understand, the president was urging everyone, to do everything they could to stay safe; until our military could neutralize those who had invaded and the new threat created by the virus.

As the days, months, and years passed, we all learned to live off the sea. My dad had saved enough food to last us months, maybe a year if we used it well. By this time, we were eating mostly fish and portioning out the remaining food her loaded. As time went by, my father and I lost my brother and my mother. My mother from a cold that never seemed to go away. TJ, my brother to a big storm that swept him overboard. I miss them both! Dad and I were living on the sea, not sure where we are but just floating about, day after day staying away from the war, and now plague stretching across all walks of earth.

One night, dad and I even noticed the animals had changed and began adapting to this scorched earth. Whales were a different color, turtles were more significant, and sharks looked like zombies, rotting, bloody, and ready to eat anything in their way. My father and I listened to the radio every night trying to hear of the hope that the world is changing, getting better, but it never did. Most days we did not hear anything, just silence from the radio. It was like the whole world had died. We would stand watch, switching off to sleep, we did that every day, to ensure that no one or nothing was going to hurt us.

One-night dad saw the first sign of life in many years, a ship off in the distance — the vast oil tanker or maybe a cruise ship. The ship was lit up like a shiny star in the distance. He woke me up with great excitement in his voice. I jumped up ready for anything but not this, a ship, what are we going to do? Is it safe, are they human, and many more questions were rolling around inside my head. After considerable discussion, my father and I decided not to run but see who or what was on this ship. As it approached all we could hope for was friendly people, and food. Any food but fish, I hated fish, I could eat anything but fish, for the rest of my life. My brother TJ and me before he died, would imagine we were in a restaurant, and we could eat any food on the menu, anything we wanted. I think it helped him and I eat most days. Most of the time we ate raw fish, not trout or salmon, but a new kind of fish none of us had seen before. We would say "what's for dinner mom... please say hamburgers, with French fries". "No! Now stop" mom would say. She never really liked our humor.

The ship drifted slowly passed us, right out of reach until it stopped. A man, stepped into view, leaned out and said "hello, anyone there? We won't hurt you!" My dad looked at me, thinking only of my future, and said: "yes, there are two of us aboard." The same man yelled back with an inflated voice, "Can I come aboard?", he had some questions for us both. My father agreed, and we both watched as the man and his crew tossed down a ladder and lowered a small rowboat.

While we waited for him, dad and I just looked at each other, with anxiety on our faces. The crisp night air stung my lungs, and the wind chilled me to the bone. We bundled up with one another, wondering if we would finally be rescued. From the time he lowered himself into the boat until he arrived, it seemed to take him only a few minutes.

When he approached, I could see his age written within the scares and wrinkles of his face. He was maybe forty-five or so. He had greying hair and a large cut across his face, has become a scare. He wore a thick black pair of pants, with big side pockets, and a wool sweater. The sweater looked dark green, with white strips. When he stepped onto our boat, dad just held my hand with a protective grip, and nicely ask who he was. "My name is Jack, and this is my ship." "This is Sam, my daughter, and I am Rick. What are you doing here, Jack?" "Well just keeping safe and looking for others like yourself. If you listened for just a moment, Rick, I would like to tell you about my ship and its passengers. During the big war, I was a marine for the United States. I fought alongside men, great men, but in the end, there was nothing my men or anyone could do to save this broken and poisonous world. I was in the Middle East when word came across the radio of people dying, changing, and killing others.

Those who lived through the war and gas were either running to stay alive or were no longer normal humans. They looked human but, had white, pale skin, eyes that sunk into their faces, and they, of course, ate everything, including other people. The US Military was called in to fight and kill off the "hybrid human population." It was not successful; many marines were killed or changed into hybrid humans. I ran, took what I could, friends, and other loved ones stole this ship and supplied it with what we needed to make a new life in this dying world. As time passed, I found many people living in these waters, trying to survive. What I would like to ask you, Rick and Sam, do you want to come aboard my ship?" Dad and I stepped out of earshot and discussed our options and agreed that it was better then what we were doing now.

"We will come aboard," dad said coughing. "Great," Jack said, "But first we must ask you a few questions and complete a physical. Our doctor needs to clear you before you can come aboard our ship". Rick and Sam agreed to his terms. Jack called up to the ship "Tom" who hung his head over and then made his way to the vessel after Jack ushered him down. "This is Sam and Rick they need a medical check before they come aboard the ship." "Hello, to you both. I will work with you separately. Rick, you first". They walked into the galley. Tom completed a physical on Rick, listening to his lungs, checked blood pressure, and asked Rick some other health questions. Next, Sam passed her father on her way into the galley. Tom was about twenty-five, good looking, and seemed friendly. He too wears the same cloths as Jack. He had dark hair and scared up the skin. She did everything Tom had asked her and met up with her father on the deck of the boat. Tom and Jack left the vessel and informed us they would discuss his findings and return shortly.

When Tom returned, he reported some good and bad news. "Sam, you are healthy and can come aboard the ship. Rick, since you have a cold, I can offer to tow your sailboat behind us until you are healthy enough to come aboard the ship. We do not know what you have, so we can't risk making everyone else aboard the ship sick."

Rick was worried about Sam's future, and taking this opportunity was what he believed was best for her. Sam tried to put up a protest against leaving her father, but she quickly lost, "You have a wonderful future ahead of you. You can make a difference in this world I know it. You are going! I will be okay and will join you when I am well" Rick said.

I was excited to board the ship, meet new people, eat other foods, and have something different to do other than sit on the sailboat. I was worried about my dad. He was sick; Tom said he would supply dad with some medicine. After saying goodbye to her father, Sam followed Jack and Tom into the small rowboat. They headed up a ladder and onto the ship.

"Sam, this is the White Cloud," Jack informed her. As I climbed up the ladder, my heart sank, at the sheer size of it. The iron ladder stung her hands as she rose. When she reached the top, the ship made her feel small. It had been the most prominent ship she had ever seen. She wondered how her choice today would impact her life moving forward. The White Cloud had a large flat-topped surface, with air vents every few feet, with ample steam pockets rushing out of them. Three doors rose above the surface of the boat, and stairs seemed to disappear beneath them.

Tom and Jack walked Sam down three stories and opened the large steel door. I felt a rush of air as the door opened, and many smells engulfed me. Not all the smells were good either I might add. Meanwhile, dad connected to the White Cloud, given food, medicine, and supplies. My dad was told in three days, he would be checked in on and provided with more supplies or if he was well, he could come aboard. Once my eyes had adjusted to the deemed lighting, I could see a long row of beds, stretching down one side, of the ship and bathrooms for both sexes, on the other side. As we walked through each corridor, I could see nothing but beds, and mid-way down one of the passages, I saw my name written on one of the top bunks. Below my name, I saw my fathers. "That's your bunk there, it's not much, but at least it's yours," Jack stated.

Tom was tasked with showing me around, explaining the rules, helping me pick out my job, where to eat, bath, and get supplies. You could get anything from cloths to medication. I, of course, was excited to see the mess hall and all the food I could order. "Sam, I want to make sure you know all the rules. Most of the rules needed in community living, but some of them you may not enjoy, but you will get used to them. If you don't follow the rules, we will ask you to leave, with or without force. Every person here must be in bunk by nine pm every day. Breakfast is at six am lunch at one pm, and dinner at six. If you miss any mealtime, you don't eat. Every day you will work at least six hours, bath and change your clothes. You can go anywhere on the ship except for the main office at the end of this corridor. Those are the officer's quarters. They are the men and women who decide where we go, what we eat, who we invite upon the ship, and whether a couple can have kids. Mainly, they keep us safe and make all the hard decisions. Do you have any questions?" Tom asked. Sam did not have any questions and agreed to the ships' rules. "The next stop is the job center" Tom said.

"Sam, you can't be picky, these are the only jobs available. If you do well, you can move up in your position or even change positions when one opens up, but you must start somewhere" Tom said. Sam looked at the board where all the open jobs were listed. The open positions are seen here, on a big corkboard in alphabetical order. Some positions open was a trash man, gardener, pet caretaker, cook, security, housekeeping, laundry maid, and many more. The one job Sam was interested in was a security officer. She wanted to learn how to protect herself and others. Help people in need, in ways she was unable to help her parents and brother. Sam felt the security position would fit her personality best. She could do this job, help others maintain security on the ship. "I think the security position. It fits who I am, and who I want to become". "Great choice, Sam," Tom said. "You will start training tomorrow, it's not easy, but I can see you doing it."

As the tour continued, Sam was able to pick out her clothes, supplies for bathing, female hygiene needs, cleaning chemicals, and bedding. Tom showed her to her storage area. The storage area was a wall of lockers, which lined the far side of each bathhouse. The cabinets continued from floor to ceiling. She put everything away and followed Tom to the dining room for dinner.

Dinner tonight was broccoli, mashed potatoes, and ham. Sam also drank a glass of goat's milk. The dinner was terrific compared to what she had been eating with her father. Sam savored every flavor and every bite. She sat alone for dinner, and her father's words were all she had on her mind. She felt so alone amongst all these people. Dinner was the first time in many years, in which Sam had a good meal, and sat with others. She needed to look forward like her mom always said before she died.

Mom would say to my brother and me how our future would be worth waiting for. What if we made it, we would want to grab our fate with both hands, not be afraid and go for it. Sam sat here thinking of her mom, dad, and TJ. She began to cry. Everything was overwhelming for her and her young life. She didn't realize how much she missed them all. Sam looked around to see if anyone had noticed that she was crying. As she looked about the room, Sam's eyes met up with a young man who was sitting on the other side of the lunchroom. He was handsome, and it made her blush. With dinner ends, and me sitting at the table by myself, I looked around, and pray for a better tomorrow.

After dinner, I found myself, walking about the ship. The ship was compartmentalized. Each area sectioned off, into different compartments. My favorite place had to be in the garden — green plants from top to bottom. Flowers are blossoming, with a sweet scent, which engaged all my senses. I could stay there all the time. It was peaceful and reminded me of home. I leaned back against a barrel of dirt and fell asleep. All night I dreamt of my family, all of us living together here on the white cloud. I knew that was not possible. As I drifted further into my dream, the sprinklers went off and awoke me with a fright. It took me a moment to remember where I had fallen asleep. I quickly ran out of the greenhouse, and towards the showers. I knew all the women and men would be waking soon, and I needed to shower before going to breakfast. When I was done, I walked out to my bunk and laid down until the alarm for breakfast would awaken me again.

No more than thirty minutes later, the alarm went off. I decided to wait until, the crowd lessened, before I got up, made my bed, and walked to the kitchen for breakfast. On my way to breakfast, I saw that same young man I meet eyes with the day before. He was about nineteen and handsome. He said hello, I was not sure what to say, "hello," he said again. All I could say was "hi..." and quickly walked away. "Man, I'm stupid, just turn around and introduce yourself!" She felt embarrassed. He was just a cute guy, saying hi. Of course, she did not get the courage to turn and say hello back. He had blue eyes, blond hair, and looked like he used to be a jock.

After breakfast, I had to find my way to the security office and start training. I walked past the tables to the kitchen and put my tray away. I looked throughout the galley to locate a map but didn't find on. It was crazy! You would think there would be a map somewhere. Once everyone had finished eating, they scattered off to their jobs. I, of course, was a deer caught in headlights, had no idea where to go. I set off to the bunks and then maybe I could find my way to the security office. On my way to my bed, I ran into an older woman, who must have seen my confusion, and she showed me to the security training room.

I opened the door and was greeted by a man in his early forties, greying hair, about six-foot-tall, and he had a scar across his face from his left ear to the bottom of his chin. "My name is Sam, and I am supposed to start work today." "Yes, I remember someone saying that last night. Hello Sam, I am Cliff. Today I will show you around, and then you will need to complete further testing before you can start the fusion process". "Okay!" Sam said with the sound of confusion in her voice. What is the fusion process she thought to herself? "Sam every day you will come to the office, get your orders, and then go to post. You will also train every day with your peers, learn how to fight, shoot, and learn ways to become invisible, like a fly on the wall. This way, you do not impact everyday life on the ship or the people who live on it. Others will learn to walk past you as if you weren't there.

"I head you earlier say something about the fusion process? What is that, Sam asked?" "It will all be explained to you soon enough. Let's get to the training facility and start your testing process. Sam followed Cliff down a series of long walkways, and down three flights of stairs. The walkways were dark, damp, and smelled like mildew. The walls looked as if they were dipped in water, covered with a light mist of water, and had a light green moss all over. When Sam and Cliff reached the bottom of the stairs, a large opening came into view. Sam could see other people, training, and preparing for the day. Cliff raised his hand and said, everyone "QUITE...." The crowd quieted down.

Sam could see people stop what they were doing, looking at Cliff. They knelt and looked up ready for whatever news he was about to present. "This is Sam, she arrived yesterday, and has chosen to become a member of the security team." Everyone welcomed her, then just turned around and went back to what they were all doing. Except, for one young man, and it happens to be the cute one from this morning. He just stood there, smiling at her.

Cliff stood in front of Sam and introduced her to Max. "Max will be doing your testing today." Sam must have looked scared because Max put his hand on her shoulder and assured her that it would be okay. Sam flinched at his touch, pulled away without saying anything, and followed Cliff and Max to another room. The room appeared to be a doctor's examination room with workout equipment added. "The first round of tests will test your agility, second will focus on health, and the third test will gauge your intelligence. "I said hi to you this morning, but you did not say anything in return." "Sorry, Max, can you just pretend that did not happen and just start over?" Max thought for a minute and said, "I guess if you will go on a walk with me tonight?"

Sam, confused, and nervous, "I just met you, why would I agree to that?" "Because that is how you get to know others.... you know talk with them, learn about one another's, likes and dislikes". "I know that, but why don't I get to know you a little more before we go on a date?" "Who said it was a date?" "Okay love birds, Cliff smiled! Let's start the testing; there is a lot to be done in one day". The agility testing was just like a P.E class, it was easy, but as the time moved from ten minutes to thirty to then forty-five. She began to tire. "Can I take a break now?" "Nope, it is part of the testing to see how you act under pressure?" A few hours had passed, and by then, Sam was exhausted. Max interjected and said, "time to begin the health testing, follow me."

The doctor, Tom, took some of Sam's blood. He took her blood pressure, heart rate again, and conducted some follow-up tests. After that, Tom sent her to begin the third and final test, which would evaluate her intelligence. The test was the hardest test Sam has ever taken. It was just like the ones at school. She and her brother would undertake an assessment each year to see what they had learned and retained. This one was worse! It had the hardest questions, and Sam was nervous! "What if I did not pass?" She said to herself. One-hour later, Sam was done and went to lunch. She felt like she had spent all day at school, on finals week.

Max walked with her, and they sat at the same table. Both Max and Sam just stared into one another's eyes for a few minutes before either could get up the nerve to talk. "Sam, how did you end up on the White Cloud?" "Where to start," she said. Sam told Max about her father, mother, and brother; and how they ended up on the white cloud. "Where is your dad now?" "He is being towed from behind the boat. He has a cold and Tom does not think he will make it". "I am very sorry," Max said. "How long has he been sick"? "Well for a while now, but dad was fighting it off well, just like my mother did. But in the end, I know he may not make it". At least I'll be the White Cloud, and not alone". "I am sorry to hear that Sam, I hope he gets better soon." "We should get back to the training room! You have more to do before quitting time."

As they entered the training room, it all fell silent. Sam looked around, (thinking to herself), it feels like the first day of school all over again, why are they staring, did I mess up the testing? Shortly after entering Cliff came around the corner and saw Sam. "Nice to see you back, do you want to come with me, we need to discuss your results?" "Okay," She said. "Max, you need to stay here." She followed Cliff into a room where the doctor stood waiting for them. "How bad was it?" she asked. "What do you mean? You scored the highest out of anyone who has ever taken this test". "WOW! How" "We are not sure, but we want to move on to the next step, which is the fusion process." "Wait, I need to know what the fusion process is first." "We cannot tell you!" It is top secret; it will change you, make you a better soldier. You must do it on that information alone or not at all. What will it be Sam?" All she could do was think about her family's sacrifices over the last year. Sam paused… if she can help others, it would be worth it. "Is it dangerous?" "To be honest, we have never done this before. It could hurt you or make you dangerous," the doc said. Without another thought,

Sam said, "I'll do it."

She was directed to undress, put on a gown, and lay on the table. Everyone left as the doctor started the process. She had three different bags hooked up to her IV. All different colors, one was yellow, one was green, and the last was almost black. As the liquid went through the IV, into her arm, it felt cold as ice, as it entered her bloodstream. The room was cold and quiet for a long time as the IV emptied. She began to feel tired, and the last thing she remembered was looking up at this old metal light hanging from the ceiling.

Hours later, she woke up. Sam noticed many things that were different about herself and her surroundings. She had more heightened senses, not just one but all of them. Sam could hear more clearly, see in more detail, and smell everything. She could see the specks of sand on her blanket, the water droplets on the ship's wall, and her long hair on her arms. It magnified everything she saw. The noise of the crowded ship began to overwhelm her ears. It seemed as if the whole ship was yelling, water splashing against the haul, and the heartbeats of her crewmates, thump, thump, thump. She could not seem to focus on anything else. Sam slowly sat up; she felt sick at first but was able to stand after a few minutes. Sam thought to herself, what am I? What have I done to myself? It took all her energy, to get up and try to walk, she just felt like a baby all over again, exploring her new world.

Max was there waiting for her when she sat up. "Max, what are you doing in here?" "I was asked to great you when you woke up, and make sure you were safe before you walk about with others on the ship." "I need a few minutes'. I feel much different than I expected." Max agreed to give her a minute alone before he walked her out to the doc. Max saw Sam with different eyes. She was so beautiful. Something in her had changed. She had big green eyes, the color of the forest, flowing red hair, and soft white skin. Every part of her was now polished, even her teeth, now white and slightly pointed.

When Sam came walking out of the bathroom, Max couldn't breathe, his heart was racing, and his mind went blank. All he could say to Sam was "your so beautiful." Sam blushed and said, thank you. Sam could hear his heart racing and see the sweat dripping from his face. "You're not so bad yourself," Sam said with a grin. Sam took Max's hand, looked at him, and said, "I am ready." She opened the door and looked upon a large open room, where she saw doc waiting for them at his desk. Doc's eyes widened and could not stop gazing at Sam's transformation. She could hear his heart pounding, between his and Max's, it was like being in a thunderstorm, but without the rain.

Chapter 2

THE CHANGE

The first night after the change was the hardest for Sam, she remembered herself screaming during the changing process, not being able to move or speak, she lost all power over herself. She was laying there, her eyes closed and wishing for it to be over. Then all at once, she awoke. After she completed a medical check, she made her way through the ship and to her bunk. She was ready for sleep, the energy needed during the fusion process, left Sam with little to stay awake on. She said her goodnights to Max and fell right to sleep.

Throughout the night, Sam kept waking up. She would feel herself slipping away into nothingness. The morning could not have come sooner. When she awoke, Max was standing by her bunk, and everyone had already left for breakfast. He, of course, could not stop looking at her, seeing the difference in her appearance, but knowing it was still the same Sam, he met almost a week ago. Max was wearing his security uniform, blue and black with a knitted picture of a white cloud on it.

The uniform was tight-fitting, made from hand-spun

sheep's wool. It was knitted tightly. It looked challenging to move in and had little give in the cloth. This must have been done on purpose to make the material more difficult to puncture in a fight. Max and the other security guards were not like Sam, she was the first they tried to change, and would not be the last. The science department had been working on the serum for almost three years now. It was a cross between the hybrid human DNA and the DNA of different mammals. The serum was developed to make her stronger than a hybrid human and less likely to become dangerous to humans. Max walked with Sam to her locker, where she was given a security guard uniform to put on before eating breakfast. She was excited to experience the whole ship with her heightened senses and abilities. Sam walked through the boat, hearing it with new ears and seeing it with fresh eyes.

She could hear the water splashing against the haul of White Cloud, and she could listen to everyone's conversations. It was hard to drown out all the noise or tell what everyone was saying, but she just needed time to figure it all out. Max just walked next to her. Sam did her best to hide what she was experiencing from him. Sam quickly picked out her breakfast and tried to find a quiet place to eat. Max continued to follow her like a shadow. Not even thinking to ask how she was feeling. Sam ate her breakfast without saying a word, she could not even think to herself, all she could hear was the noises around her.

Max, growing suspicious, finally asked her, "Did I do something wrong?" "No, it is hard to be in here with all these people and all the noise," she snapped. She also wondered, "could I learn to control all the noise?" She felt, what's the word, anxious about being different, the concern that others would eventually fear her. This project was top secret, but others would finally notice her physical changes. What would she tell people and those she grew closer to. While eating, Sam had more memories. They began to appear to her, like a movie screen playing out her life. Everything, from her current situation moving backwards to her childhood. She could remember her first breath, the first time she walked and talked. Her first birthday when mom gave her a big red ball, and her first word. Every aspect of childhood, she now remembered. The more she remembered about her family and life. The sadder she became. She would never see any of them again, never walk to school with her brother, or go to the movies with her mom or play ball with her dad. The thoughts just kept flowing in, she finally had to excuse herself from breakfast and go back to her bunk.

It did not take long before Max walked through the hall towards her. Max approached her slowly, she looked up at him, with tears flowing from her eyes, "what is happening to me? I am scared," she told him. "Max I have memories from when I was born, I can hear everything, except for my own thoughts, and my eyes, there...there different too". "It will be okay, Sam! I promise." "We should go see the doc," Max stated. "Okay, can I just sit here with you for a minute?" "Yes! As long as you need Sam, I am here". She pressed her face against his chest, taking in his smell, and listening to his heartbeat as she let go of her pain. It did not take long before she had dozed off to sleep.

Max allowed her to sleep for as long as he could. He knew that she needed to see the doc and start training. Jack would not like them being late for daily activities. Max slowly stirred Sam awake. "We really need to get going. Are you feeling better?" "Yes, a little thank you for being here." Sam slowly woke up and followed Max to the infirmary. Doc was working with someone else when they arrived. Sam and Max waited for him outside. Sam continued to lean on Max while they waited. She was beside herself at what she was feeling, sensing, and hearing. She hoped doc would have some ideas for her, anything that would lesson, the bombarding of thoughts, feelings, senses, and noise. Doc opened the door and invited Sam inside. "Sam is everything alright?" "What is going on" Tom (doc) asked. Sam again explained everything to the doc.

She told him about her worries, and ask what she needs to do, to control her senses. Tom, taking notes like he always did, looked up at her with surprise, "Everything happening to you is amazing! I know it is overwhelming for you now, but in time it will improve. I wish there were something I could say to make it better, but I can't. I am just fascinated with the change and your health". Sam, he said softly "to be honest we have never created anything like yourself, that means the only person that can learn to control how you feel, is you! You should write in a journal daily, release all the pain you are feeling, and describe the abilities you are experiencing. This may help me understand how to help you. This will be a long process, Sam. The training will just increase your stress and abilities. You will start training tomorrow you should rest up; this way you, are ready to start tomorrow. How does that sound Sam?" Sam thought about what he said, this was all new to them as well as herself. Sam agreed to try.

She grabbed a notebook from the doc, and both Sam and Max left. The rest of the day was a blur. She remembered just walking about the boat with Max. Neither of them talking, just being with one another. Sam could not control the noise bombarding her senses, she did not want to even speak. Max, respected that, and also took dinner to her, upon the deck. Being on the deck was much quieter for Sam. She listened to the noise of the water, and wind as it blew her hair about. She was grateful to Max, he just sat with her until the sun began to set. She fell asleep, watching the sunset in the distance.

When she awoke, she started writing down her dreams and decided to focus on quieting the noise of the ship and crew. Max came up to the deck shortly after she had finished writing. He brought her breakfast, and as they watched the sunrise. After she and Max ate, they went for a run since no one was awake on the ship yet. After their run, both Max and Sam took a shower and meet up by her bunk. "Max, what do we do every day working in security? Do we ever go on land?" Max looked at her with surprise in his face. "We never go on land, it is too dangerous for us, we would be killed, and then the hybrids would know the location of White Cloud. As security officers, we are assigned to a different security rotation daily, every day is different, rotating our shifts and locations. It may seem that every day is the same, but it is not. There are days we find new people lost, we find hybrids on boats looking for people, and we must be ready for that, and there are in boat problems such as fights among crew members. You will learn every detail of this during training, and you have to know each assignment by heart before you start being assigned alone. I will be your instructor until you have learned all I can teach you". Sam thought in silence for a moment, and then said, "It sounds wonderful! Let's get to work then!"

Chapter 3

TRAINING

Training started early, Sam was excited and nervous all at the same time. She was ready for it, though, sitting around and waiting for something to do was getting a little redundant. Although the day of sleep and rest was very needed. She continued to have memories of her childhood and her parents. She could remember a time when they were all fighting over a game of Uno, and what the rules were. It was a fight, but she wanted nothing more than to see her family again. No matter if they were fighting or not, at least she would have them back.

Sam met Max after her shower. "What is the plan for today, Max?" Sam asked, "We are going to go over the policies, and procedures of the ship, the ship's layout, protocols, and weapons training." "Okay, none of that sound fun to me except for the weapons training" Sam said. "Yes, true, but at least we can hang out together all day!" "Funny! You're a joker, aren't you?" She asked. "Yes, I find that making others laugh, helps me heal from all of my pain, and the pain I see in others." "That was a deeper response then I expected" she said. "Yep, that is me!"

Max responded. Sam and Max laughed and started working on the paperwork side of training. It took about four hours. Sam hated the paperwork. She struggled to stay focused, with the noise all around her. On the bright side, Sam was able to remember everything they read, talked about, and watched. It was easy for her like she had been doing this job her whole life. It was as if her brain had become more developed and had more capabilities, then it ever did before.

Gun training was terrific, the shooting range was in a large room. The walls had a hard protective, material over them, it was set up to protect the ship from bullets. The room had an extensive electronic system, which projected images on the walls. The images included hybrid humans and obstacles she needed to surpass. Every bullet coming out of the gun Sam could hear. From the ball hitting the chamber, the ignition of the gun, and the exit of the shell. She went through the exercise faster than anyone else on the team and receiving the highest score. She did not feel tired, she was not even sweating, Max could not believe it. "Sam, that was amazing! Have you ever used a gun before?" "No never, just seen it done on T.V shows, but never imagined doing it," She replied. After Sam had finished the gun course, it was time for lunch.

She and Max walked together to the kitchen. Everyone from the ship was there, taking a much-needed break from work. Sam's newest friend Alice walked up to them. "Hey Sam, do you guys want to come to eat with the rest of the gang and me?" Sam and Max followed her to the table after ordering their lunches, Hamburgers with rice and peas. Alice was Cliff's daughter, and she had been on the ship for many years now. She and Nigel, 'Jack's son, have grown up together and are now a couple. Alice was a funny, outgoing type of girl. She had flowing red hair, freckles all over, and big blue eyes. Sam could see why Nigel liked her so much. Alice and her father ran a fishing boat before the war broke out. They were out at sea when the bombs started falling from the sky, and after a few years, they too found the White cloud and were welcomed by Jack.

Nigel, on the other hand, was a scrappy young man, black hair, and deep brown eyes. He was brought aboard the ship after his father found him. His dad Jack was at war when he and his mother ran from place to place, trying to stay away from the changing human's. Nigel talked about them once, he said it was like the people became animals, they lost all humanity, using their strength, and speed to run down everyone they could. Nigel was there when his mother was changed into a hybrid. He never really talked about what happened, he still dreamed about the attack. Sam, Nigel asked, "How is training going so far?" "It has been very tiring for me mostly. The gun training came the easiest and most fun, of course." "I wish I could do that job, but when I came on the ship, it was not a choice, and my father wanted me, to help him with the computer systems, not security. Now I get to watch everyone on a screen, all day. My daily excitement comes from watching the lives of everyone on the ship". Nigel said. "Nigel, you are good at your job, and the security team has a fun job. I just hang out with the plants all day, and harvest when needed." Alice sighed. "No matter what, we all have different jobs, and we each play a role in how the ship runs," Max said.

"It is time to get back to work," Sam said as the bell rang. "I want to get together with you later, Alice!" "I will find you after dinner," she replied. Sam wanted to talk with Alice, about Max's behavior lately and her developing feelings for him. She liked Max, but if those feelings grew, someone could use them against her. Use Max as leverage. Sam was afraid to get close to another person, she can eventually lose. With her advancing skills, she is worried that one day they will want to use her as a weapon. Sam does not want that to happen, but when that time comes, will she have a choice?

Chapter 4

IDENTITY

Sam completed her first day of training as a security guard and has been a hybrid for a few weeks now. Each day brings about new challenges and sacrifices. Sam has continued concerns about Max's behavior and his advances towards her. She made time to talk with Alice about her worries. "How can I get close to him if I don't even know who I am? I am changing, and that alone scares me?" Sam asked Alice, making sure not to tell her about the serum. "Sam, you can't possibly know that right now. You have only been with us for a few weeks, give it some time. You will learn as you go, and you will know who you are on time. Don't worry about what's going to happen, just focus on each day. All of us will help you through this." Alice scolded. "When it comes to Max, just let it happen, Sam. Yes, you have had losses but so have everyone, of us who lives on this ship Sam. Remember that! None of us come without the baggage of the past, nor can we change who we are right now".

"I get what you are saying Alice, I do, but what if I hurt him or any of you? I am afraid of losing you all, as this new person is growing over the old one. I don't want Max to become collateral damage" she said. "Sam, we know who you are and what you have taken on to become a fighter in this war. We take on the responsibility of what happens to us in the process." "Let me get this right, what you are saying Alice is that I am just overthinking it all and need to let it come, one day at a time?" "Yes! Exactly Sam!" "That is not easy for me. Especially now that I am changing. I have so many things to work on within myself, I don't know how to turn off my worry, Alice". "Just talk to him, Sam, let Max make his own choices. You have just met and started liking who you saw in each other". "I will try, Alice."

"By the way, how has your day been Alice?" "My day? Let's see, I have been tending to the plants, and listening to old Roxie boss me around and tell me how I am doing everything wrong. She has been working in the garden too long and thinks that plants will grow in here the same way they grew on the land. I have been a botanist and scientist for a few years now, and there is, way more to growing in the dark then she thinks." "Alice, it sounds very frustrating for you, can't you just keep on doing it your way?" "No Sam, she is still the boss, and I can still get into trouble if I don't do things the way they want them done." "What does Nigel think about it?" Sam asked. "He tells me to just suck it up, buttercup! He works with his father all day long, and there is no way Roxie is worst than that". Both laughing, Sam and Alice notice the time. "It is just about bedtime. We need to go get ready for bed, Sam," Alice stated.

Sam and Alice strolled to the woman's bathing chamber, both longed for the hot water and the relaxing sound the water makes as it flows over their heads and shoulders. The water rushed over Sam's body, releasing the tension of the day, in her shoulders, and the lines of her face. Sam tried not to think of what Alice, and she discussed it. Instead, she focused on the water, hitting her head. She got lost within herself while she was bathing.

The bell rang out overhead. It was meant to tell them it was bedtime. It was such a shock that Sam jumped with fright. The rest of the women, in the bathing chamber, stared at her and began laughing. "You will get used to it in time," an older woman to the left of her said. Sam still shaken by the loud ringing, got dressed, and headed to her bunk. She is still not sleeping well. Every time Sam fell asleep, she could feel the inner animal, trying to emerge. It was like having dreams, but she was within them, not watching them. Sam could feel the urge to hunt and feed. She could smell the sweat dripping off each person's brow, smell the minty soap they all used, and hear their beating hearts as they slept. She could feel herself being drawn to them, like one magnet to another. This scared her every time, and she awoke, over and over. She knew deep inside; she did not want to hurt anyone on the ship or jeopardize everything her father died for. This one chance of a healthy life within this poisoned world.

Sam must of, fallen asleep because when she awoke again, Max was looking down at her. "What are you doing Max" "You were sleeping. I did not want to wake you". "Well, I am awake now" "Sam, we have to meet up with doc today and continue your training." "Okay! I did not sleep well again last night. I kept having nightmares, and I am just not in a great mood. I can get ready and head to breakfast with you, Max". Sam considered talking with Max on their way to breakfast, but she could not find the words.

During breakfast, Alice introduced us to her brother Jackson and her coworker Sue. Jackson reminded Sam of her younger brother. He was about sixteen, full of wild spirit, and looked like a little boxer. Jackson had brown hair, a scar from his shoulder blade to his cheekbone, and he had deep blue eyes. He always brought laughter to the table, stories of all the things he had done, how he was the smartest security guard aboard the ship. All of us would just laugh at his young ego. Sam was only a few years older, but she felt much wiser than Jackson.

Sue was older than Sam, she was the oldest of them, and brought a wise spirit. She had long blond hair with big green eyes. Sue worked with Alice and was a trainer for some of the other positions on the boat. She knew the ends and outs of all the jobs. Sam had met her during her first few days on the ship, and she was the one who helped her through her father's death. "How has the new job been Sam?" Sue asked. "It has been going well, its been a hard adjustment for me, but overall, I am learning a lot about the job and myself." "That is great, Sam. I think we are going to port soon. We need some supplies, and we have to forage for them." Sue said.

"That is not something my dad wants everyone to know! People would try to leave the ship for fresh air, and we would end up losing them to the hybrids. Let's not talk about this now," Nigel scolded. "This is a surprise to me," Sam said. "I thought we never did that? It is too dangerous. My dad and I tried that once, and it was a crazy experience for us. I almost lost him then." "Sam don't worry about it, it is not something, we do" Max reassured her.

After breakfast, her friends left Sam and Max alone to walk the training room. Sam again wanted to talk with him about everything but the talk about going ashore caught her by surprise. "Max, why would they risk going ashore?" "When they do it is normally for medicine we need and have run out of, or just to keep our security teams ready for a fight. We have you, they may want to see how well you do in combat". "Max, I am not ready for that, I am still trying to manage all my senses and impulses." "Don't worry Sam, that's why we are going to see the doc, he will not allow them to take you out if you are not ready, and neither will I." The rest of the way to doc's office Sam was even more nervous now, knowing that the team may be counting on her to get them through whatever may happen out there. After all, Sam just met her side, and trust has not been built yet.

When they reached the doc's office. "I'm here what do you need, from me today?" "Hello Sam, why don't you come with me?" "Yeah, of course," "Sam, how have you been doing?" "Doc I'm not really sure. I have been writing everything down like you asked me to, but some new things are going on". "What is new Sam?" "Last night, I really struggled with sleep. I kept having what I think is a dream, but it seems more real than that. I feel a sense of hunger, I sense everyone around me, feel their heart beats, and have the urge to eat everyone. I not sure what is happening to me doc, I know that I would never hurt anyone, but part of me wants to". "Sam that is very worry some to me as well. Why don't I run some tests, and keep you under observation for tonight?" "If that is what you think. I just don't know who I am anymore, doc". "Sam, you are the same girl that came to live with us, just weeks ago, but now your stronger.

No matter what, you have the same loving and kind heart, you have always had. That is why I chose you. You are kind and would not hurt others in anger. This will help you fight the urges you are now experiencing." "I am trusting you the doc, I hope you are right! When should I come back tonight for observation?" "Why don't you let me run some blood work now and then you can come back after dinner." "I guess, whatever you say doc." Doc, instead of drawing her blood, tranquilized her.

The last thing Sam remembered was seeing the look of regret on the doc's face. She was going to get her blood work done, and then what happened? Sam could not remember. She awoke on a small motorboat heading towards the shore. Her eyes were struggled to focus on anything, her head hurt, and Sam could see as if it were still day time, even though she knew it was night. She smelled the salty sea air and the scent of death. Sam saw a full moon and a sky full of stars. The boat was small, with some kind of tarp, for camouflage. Sam could hear the motor humming and water splashing into the boat. She saw three other men sitting with her in the boat, all in full combat gear.

She was the only one that did not have night vision on. One of the men was Max! "Max, what happened? I thought you said you would protect me? Where are we going?" "I am sorry Sam there was nothing I could do. I wish I had a choice in the matter, but I didn't. We are on our way to the harbor we need some medical equipment and other supplies. Doc did not want to scare you, and he wanted to see how you would adapt to stress tonight, not just for his research but for you." "How is this for me, Max? I was drugged and brought out here with you guys, no warning just forced to do it. I did not sign up for this". Oscar, the captain of her team, said, "It does not matter what happened, you are here with us, and are here to help. Let us focus on the mission and get back to the ship safe".

Sam could see Rex, who was another member of her team sitting next to Oscar. "Fine, Sam said I'll do this but will be talking with doc when we get back. Where is my gear?" "You are wearing it, Sam!" "Really? Who dressed me?" "I did," Max said. Embarrassed, Sam looked up at Oscar, "what is the plan, and what is my role here exactly?" "We are going to do a water entry in ten minutes, that will keep the boat away from the shore, and us give us about a fifteen-minute swim. Once we reach the shore, there is a medical supply warehouse, about two miles in. We will have you run the point, this way you will be able to sense the dark ones or see them before we are ambushed. We will work as a team, quietly, and swiftly. Any questions?" "I have so many, but I think I understand what I am to do. If we are ambushed, how do I keep us safe?" "Sam, just by staying alert and acting quicker than us. Doc thinks that you will not be affected by bites or scratches. Hopefully, that means you won't turn and can keep them off us. We have new bullets that will blow up our targets and prevent them from continuing to attack. We will use fewer bullets this way. From here on out I need silence." Oscar said.

Sam had so many thoughts in her mind. She had only seen the hybrids many years earlier. Sam's dad and Sam attempted to get supplies ashore. It was scary then, and now they have had more time to adapt and change. What about the animals? She remembers the monster-like animals from her time on the sailboat. They could be walking into anything, she needed to focus on her senses. The engine slowed to a stop, and the anchor was dropped. Oscar used hand signals to motion for them to enter the water.

They quietly slipped into the water and started swimming. The bay was cold as ice, it took Sam's breath away, the minute she hit the water. Sam had to take a few deep breaths before she could swim. It did not take Sam but a minute or two to get quite a bit further to shore than her team. She had to stop and wait for them a few times. The water seemed much different to her than what it used to be. It was dark, had a stronger salt taste, and was more of a red than a blue or green.

Sam looked towards the shore and could see something moving behind a car. She could not tell what it was, her eyes were burning from all the salt in the water. Sam motioned to her crew and pointed to the shore. Oscar looked and did not seem worried, she continued swimming the rest of the way, stopping briefly to wait on them. Sam reached the beach. First, she did not see any movement or hear anything, other than her own men. When they reached the shore, Sam motioned for directions, and she continued to lead the team. Oscar handed her a map with their location marked on it and their destination. Sam starting walking towards the medical supply warehouse.

The smell throughout the town was horrible. Sam could only smell death, blood, and sewage. The buildings looked overgrown with vines and moss. Some of the buildings were starting to break down with decay. It was like walking through an abandoned town, which no one had lived in for many years. She could not see what town they were in or identify the state. With buildings falling down around her, she did not know how to find her bearings. Sam began to feel uneasy as if someone or something was watching them from afar. Sam motioned for the team to stop, as she looked around. Sam started to look in all directions, using her enhanced sight, and smell to help her identify what was lurking about. It was an animal, maybe a wolf, or a large dog. With a tall person standing beside it. By the time she pointed towards the object, the object was gone.

Oscar wanted her to continue moving, they were only about five blocks away from the warehouse, and the daytime was coming fast. They did not want to be out when the sun came up. Continuing towards the warehouse, Sam, continued to feel like something was watching them. She could sense a presence she did not understand. Sam again attempted to stop her team, but they continued to push her forward. How could she protect them if they don't start listening to her directions?

Suddenly, Sam began to feel hot, followed by a burning sensation throughout her body, like her whole body was on fire. Her bones started to pop, move, and take shape. One bone at a time-shifting and moving into a different form. At the same time, her team stepped back, staring at her with mouths open and concern within their eyes. She began to scream in pain, and after a short few minutes, she had transformed into a panther.

Chapter 5

COMBAT

"Sam, Sam" she heard Max say, you look like an enormous black panther. Sam could feel the fear radiating off her team. She no longer felt human, she had four big paws, a long tail and enormous head. Sam had no idea what to do or how to do it. She could sense everything around her. Sam could smell a rotting smell coming off the intruders just up the hill. Sam looked up the hill towards the stench of death, and there stood many dark ones and what looked like their wolves.

Within a blink of an eye, she was gone, running, racing to attack whoever was waiting for them. The faster she ran, the further she got away from her team. She instinctively knew where to attack and how. She collided with a dark one and found its throat. She began ripping at its throat with her enormous jaws. Bloodshot out everywhere, like a damn had opened. One of the wolves jumped in and tried to take a bite out of Sam. She veered to the left and bit the neck of another hybrid. While killing one, there was another. Each getting a bit in before falling to the ground with a thud. The taste of blood encouraged her to engorge on the taste of their bodies. Going from one to another. Max had finally reached her position and began shooting the dark ones and wolves she had not killed yet. One explosion after another, left each body mangled, and their guts all over Max.

The rest of Sam's team approached her slowly, eyes on her, with continued fear. What she had done was unbelievable. All the dark ones were dead in a matter of minutes, and Sam only had a few bites visible on her. She was covered in blood, which made her look even more fearsome to her team. "Sam? Max said with caution, is that you?" She looked up at them and had to fight her instincts to attack. The taste of blood made her hungry for more. She was surprised to find out that she could talk, "It's me Max." "Are you okay, Sam?" "I think so, yes. I don't really know what happened. I just changed when I felt the dark ones." "That was gruesome to watch. Do you think you can stay in this form until we are done?" Oscar asked. "I don't know," Sam said, "but I will try." Sam and the team rejoined their formation with Sam as the lead. They were able to enter and leave the warehouse without any other attempts at their lives. Once Sam and her team reach the boat, all of them seemed to sighed with relief. They all made it due to Sam's abilities.

"Sam, we will be home soon, do you think you can try to change back into your human form?" Oscar asked. "I am not sure I know how to, but if I do, I will need some new clothes first. I don't want to be naked in from of you men". "Good point," Oscar stated. "You can wait till we board the ship. Max can bring you some clothes, and you can try to change then. I don't want people fearing or seeing you." Sam agreed, knowing that seeing a bloody, large panther would scare all the people on the ship. She just laid down to lick her wounds, all the way back to the White Cloud. Sam now knew who Sam was, but this also meant she could be used as a weapon in this war. She would do everything she could to prevent that from happening, even if that meant leaving the White Cloud, and Max.

Chapter 6

NEXT PLEASE

After the rest of her team left the boat, Sam grabbed the cloths Max had gathered for her and attempted to change back. She sat there staring at the beautiful stars, thinking of her family and how proud they must be, looking down on her from heaven. At that moment, Sam began to change back to her human form. Her bones breaking, moving back into place, and the worse part was the pain she felt as her bones broke and moved. Shortly after, Sam entered the White Cloud, ascending the same stairs Sam did the night Sam arrived. There she found Max waiting for her. "Doc wants to see you, Sam." "I really don't want to see him right now, I am going to the showers and will be out in a while." Sam was too angry at him and too bloody to see anyone. She took her time in the shower, rinsing off all the bits, and blood. She counted eight bites spread throughout her body. Some were deeper than the others, but the pain was minimal. She hoped doc was right, and she would not change into a dark one, only time would tell. Doc would want her under observation for the next twenty-four hours. She knew this, but she took her time anyways, getting dressed, and ready to go meet with him. She was mad at him after all. He could have told her the truth, but he chose to lie to her instead. "Thanks for waiting for Max" "Remember Sam, everything that happened is top secret, you can't tell Alice or the others, understand?" "I understand that Max, I hate that you even know, and can see what I have become. I like you Max, but how can anyone be with an animal? I can't trust myself with you or anyone else now". "Sam, yes you can, you controlled it then, and you will continue to. I like you too, and do not plan on stopping any time soon. Go ahead and try to push me away, I am glued to you".

Sam gave him a disgusted look and walked the rest of the way to the doc's office in silence. She was hoping that her anger at doc wouldn't trigger her change and attack him. As they approached his office, Sam could sense that he was not alone, and whoever was in that room wanted a piece of Sam. There is no one else of her kind, and now she was a prize. "Come on in Sam, Max," the doc said. "There are a few others here who want to talk with you." Sam entered the room, she could see Jack, doc, Oscar, Rex, and a woman that She did not know. "I am Evelyn, and I run and make all the decisions on this ship." She extended her hand to meet Sam's. Sam did not like her, did not even need to shake her hand, but knew she better, it would not look good to refuse. "Hi, Evelyn I am Sam, it is nice to meet you. Why are all of you here?" "Whenever a military excursion takes place, we do what is called a debrief afterward. Evelyn said. "We also needed to check in with you and make sure you understand what top-secret means." "Evelyn, I understand what it means, and what happened won't leave this room." "Good to know, but we are not staying in this room, follow me." Evelyn led the way back out of the doc's office and ascended a set of stairs, that lead to a red door at the end of the long corridor. Once the door opened, Sam could smell the sea and a light above a small table in the corner of the room. The room had a window opened to the outside. It was open just enough for her to smell the sea. It had pink curtains, hung on black walls. The walls also had moisture dripping from them. In the room sat one desk, and two large sofas', both pink as well. Evelyn must like pink, it was everywhere. She closed the door behind them and locked it. This made Sam's heart pump faster, and Sam had to slow it down, she did not want to change in front of this woman.

"Talk to me, Oscar, what happened?" Evelyn said. "The trip was a success we were able to get in and out with no casualties. Sam was able to destroy them before they even had a chance to attack us." "Sam, how were you able to take them out so quickly?" "What? Didn't the guys tell you already?" "No, they did not and do not talk to me like that, just answer the question Sam." Sam again had to take a deep breath before she began. "Once we landed, I could sense that someone or thing was watching us, Oscar pushed us forward. Once we were about five or six blocks away from the warehouse, there they stood. The dark ones with huge wolves at their sides. Something happened within me, and I changed into a large black panther, I took off towards them, and killed them all before they could hurt the team. Max killed two of the wolves." "Wait! You changed into an animal? Did you get bit?" asked Evelyn. "Yes, I changed, and yes, I got a bit! Doc says I should be fine. I figured that is why he wanted to see me and put me under observation for twenty-four hours." "This is big! I can't believe the serum worked and you changed like that" Stated Evelyn. Evelyn sat at her desk for a few minutes in silence, not with worry on her face but surprise.

"Okay, this does not leave the room, no one can know that Sam changes into an animal, nor do the damage that she did. Doc runs some tests and keep her under observation for twenty-four hours if nothing happens, and she is fine then let her out. Continue training and go about like nothing happened". "Yes, Mam," everyone said but Sam. Sam, doc and her team left the room, but Jack and Evelyn stayed behind. "Evelyn, what are you planning? We are in this together, and I need to know?" "Just because you want to know Jack, does not mean I am going to tell you anything. I am going to do what is best for this ship and the experiment. Which the board and I have developed!" "My son lives on this ship with me, and I am responsible for them all" Jack said. "That may be true, but I am your boss, and what I say goes, do you get that soldier?" "Yes, Mam." With that said, Jack left the room. He was not going to let that woman or anyone else take this ship and the people within it.

Sam followed doc back to his office. "Sam I am sorry I had to tranquilize you, I had my orders too." "Doc, I understand that, but I am still mad at you. Do what you need to do and let's get this over with." Doc took three veils of blood before Max escorted Sam into a separate quarantine room and locked her in. "I will bring you dinner in a little while, Sam" Max said. Sam was finally alone, and she finally felt isolated and excluded from everyone.

The door shut behind her, and the small room began to close in on her. It looked like a surgical room, cold, surprisingly clean, with big lights hovering over a bed. Sam did not find comfort in this. She found an air vent on the floor and curled up on it. Sam hoped that sleep would bring her comfort. She sat quietly trying to get Evelyn out of her mind, but no matter how hard she tried, she could not stop thinking about her. Evelyn appeared innocent, but deep down, She was evil. Sam knew this, but for now, she needed to keep it to herself.

Chapter 7

MAX

When Max reached the kitchen, all their friends had gotten dinner and had begun to eat. "Hey, Max, where is Sam?" Alice asked. "She is with Doc for the night, I am going to bring her dinner" Said Max "Is she okay?" Sue asked. "Yeah she is, just having some more dreams, and he wants to complete a sleep study with her." "Can you stay and eat with us?" Alice asked Max. "Yes, I will eat with you guys, just give me a minute, and I will be right over." Max got his dinner and went to sit with his friends.

His mind, though, continued to focus on Sam's welfare. He was worried about her. She will fight Jack and Evelyn she is not a soldier, and he was concerned about what that might mean for her. The rest of them knew their place, knew what could happen if they ever crossed Evelyn or Jack. Sam, on the other hand, is nothing like him and their friends. She had nothing to lose and could survive without the help of others. Max wanted to protect her in the ways he could never protect his mother and sister.

His mother had died shortly after the war started, and his sister did not make it too much longer. That's when

Jack had found him. Jack has been like a father to him, and he would be forever grateful. Max lived in Mississippi, with his mother Jude and younger sister Jasmine. When the war began, it took its time getting to Max and his family. His mother decided to move them to a camp with other survivors, hoping it would provide additional security to them if the dark ones attacked. She was hoping the US military would come to help and protect them, but no one did. Time was not on their side. It was not long before the dark ones began to attack and take members of the encampment. Not all at once but in waves. The camp did well, the first few waves of attacks. They only took a few members, but the final wave of dark ones took everyone from the camp, including Max's family. That day Max lost his mother and sister, and it has haunted him ever since. That day he and his family were eating dinner together. When the camp siren went off. Jude ushered her children out the back of the building, and towards the woods. She wanted to protect them and hoped the woods would add additional camouflage. She was wrong! About one mile out of camp, the dark ones began coming towards them from all sides. Jude hid her children in an open, hollowed-out log. She told Max to take care of his sister and that she loved them always. Jude left them, running and yelling. She hoped this act of love would save them from the dark ones and only taking her life, not theirs. Shortly, after leaving her children, Max and Jasmine watched their mother die. Max did his best to keep his sitter quiet. He turned his attention to their hiding place and trying to keep his sister quiet, or they both would die. The log they were in was damp, dark, and had numerous bugs crawling about. Max had an easier time staying quiet. He was also further back in the log and had more coverage. Jasmine, on the other hand, was not sitting still nor staying quiet. She did not like the bugs and was crying over the loss of her mother. Max tried to keep her quiet, but before he could calm her down enough, a dark one grabbed her backpack and pulled her out. Max did his best to help her, but he had to run, or he wouldn't have made it either. Max hated the memories of his family, and the dreams were just as bad. Jack found Max about one week later in Greenville, looking for food. Jack took him in and helped him overcome what happened to his family. He always wanted to go look for his sister, but Jack continued to tell him, "they are dead or changed by now."

Max did not realize how long he had been focused on his memory. He had forgotten about the conversations around him. "Max, are you okay," Alice asked. "You sat down to eat with us but have not been talking to us. What happened, this is not like you!" She asked. "I am just worried about Sam. I was just thinking about her and how I got here. I just hope she can let me in and that I can protect her for what is to surely come". "She will be okay; she is stronger than you think. Go take her dinner, and we can catch up with you both in the morning," Sue said. Max took his leave and headed to the kitchen. The kitchen was slowing down now, Max only had to wait a few minutes before the counter person came to take his order. There stood a balding older man, with an apron on over his grey shirt. "What can I get you now? You know the rules only one serving each person". "It is not for me. I am taking one plate to doc, and one to Sam. Both of which are in his office still. Jack told me you would understand and allow it. Call him if you must". "No need to bother him, I will get you two plates. Give me ten minutes to make them up".

"Thank you for being understanding, I will let Jack know how generous you were to me." Laughing, the bald man turned around and walked into the kitchen. The cafeteria had two big serving tables. One for cold food like salads, and one for hot commonly served meals. The kitchen was massive, it had three grills, and four fryers, its own fridge and freezer, sinks, and dishwasher. Three cooks and four servers worked there at any given time. The man came to the counter with two plates and the silverwear "Make sure you bring these back in the morning, or I will have your neck." Max just nodded and started walking to the doc's office.

By the time Max reached the office, it was almost eight pm, and the doc had begun dozing off. "Doc here is a dinner plate for you and Sam. Can I give it to her?" "How did you get away with that?" "I told the man that Jack approved it. The cook did not question it." "You could get into trouble if Jack finds out you did that." "Well, who cares I wanted you both to get dinner. Can I take it to her and sit for a while?" "You can give it to her, but you cannot stay with her tonight. It could be dangerous". "Fine, I guess this will have to do then." Max gave doc his plate and walked over to the observation window to check on Sam. Max looked around throughout the room, but he could not find her. "Doc, I need to go in, I can't see her anywhere." "That can't be right, let me see." Both of them began looking through the window and again at the monitors but could not find Sam. "This does not make any sense. Let's go in with tranquilizers, just in case". Max and doc slowly opened the door and walked in. Guns ready, eyes open, they entered the room and heard a deep growl. Both were startled and jumped. "Sam, it's us, we have brought you food," Max said. With no response, they turned on the lights to find her. She was no longer in human form and had turned into a giant panther. She was no more than five feet from them. She was as black as night, with green eyes, and a few white hairs on her paws. She growled again, this time they could see her teeth showing and saliva dripping from her mouth. "Its Max and doc, I am going to put your plate down, and we will leave, please don't make us tranquilize you." With no response from Sam, they put her food down and slowly stepped out the door. Doc locked the door and went to the monitors.

"She must be able to blend into the darkness, and that is why we did not see her" doc stated. "Last night, she talked to us, as if she were in human form. Tonight, she isn't, she is acting like a real panther. Why?" "I am not sure, Max, we should watch her for a few minutes." Sam began to eat, and when she was finished, she looked up at them. The life in Sam's eyes slowly came back to her, and she was able to speak again. "What happened? I just woke up eating," Sam said with concern and groggy-ness in her voice. Max and doc sighed with relief, "You had us worried for a moment there! You tried to attack us when we brought you food" Max said. "I must have been sleeping. What am I going to do? I can't sleep in the bunks if I change throughout the night!" "I don't know Sam. We will talk it over and be back soon" doc stated.

Max and doc left the room, they wanted to make sure she was unable to hear them converse. "What are we going to do doc? Should we take this to Jack or Evelyn?" "Not Evelyn, but we should find Jack and see what he thinks." Max and doc walked through the boat and to Jack's office, "Jack, can we come in? Are you here?" They said in unison. Jack looked up from some paperwork he was working on "sure, to what do I owe this occasion?" "As you know, Sam is under observation tonight. Max went to dinner and brought some dinner back for her and me, and when he took the food to her, she had changed into her panther form. We are concerned! What if she were to change overnight in the general population, she could frighten others or even attack them. What should we do? Jack"

"Wow! That is a problem. Did she know who you were when you walked in?" "No, she was still asleep, and we could not even see her till the lights were on" stated doc. "Can we just make her a bunk in the storage area of the ship for now? Max's security team is the only one who has access to that portion of the boat". "That will put her far from Max and the team, what if something were to go wrong? They are the only ones who can know what is happening" questioned Jack. "Okay, why not portion out the storage room, one for me and the guys and the other for Sam?" Max asked. "That will work if the doc can put up cameras, facing the door and the room. That way, everything is supervised. Max why don't you and doc get the plans drawn up, and have it built. She can stay in with doc until it is finished." "I can do that. It might take doc and me some time, but it will get done".

With that being said, Max and doc left Jack in his office. They walked through the ship to the storage area, which was the main cargo hold. The cargo hold was pitch black, doc and Max could not see anything, "Ouch, I walked into something. Doc where's that dang light!" They ran their hands against the hull of the boat until doc found the light. When it came on both Max and doc gasped, the cargo hold was packed full of personal belongings, for everyone who lived in the ship. "What are we going to do with all this stuff?" Max asked. "I am not sure! It sure is packed in here! I can't even see the other end of the room".

There was stuff packed from floor to ceiling. It smelled of mold and had a massive amount of stagnant air about it. "This will take us all day Max! There should be an opening at the back of the room, let's get ourselves pushed back there to open it up". "Get some air in here! That would be a good start," Max said. They could see one area, through the middle, which had a small walking space from front to back. They decided to start trying to squeeze their way through. While they worked their way through, they could see all types of items from books, to kitchen wear. Everything in the hold was brought in by crew members. None of it is allowed to be used, on the ship. "They must have put it all down here because it was easier than finding room elsewhere," said Max" "None of this is allowed Max, I am amazed it was not thrown overboard." Finley, they reached the back of the room.

There was a massive door, it could fit a small sailboat through when open. It opened outwards, both Max and the doc decided to try and open it up. When the cargo door opened, a rush of air and spray of water came pouring through. It was about eleven, almost midnight, they could look up and see the moon, and stars. It was a clear and dark night. The moon was high in the sky, half covered by encroaching clouds. No, land or lights in sight.

Neither knew what to expect when they went through all this stuff. Both men stood there, taking in the fresh night air. "Shall we get started, Max?" "How do you want to do this doc? Should we just throw it all overboard, or keep what could come in handing further down the road?" "Why don't we keep any combat-ready items, food that is not expired, the family pictures and throw the rest overboard." They began going through it one box at a time. It was harder than they thought it would be to go through the lives of others. Finding happy family pictures, wondering if any of them were still alive or had they died. The kid's art pictures and projects were the worst for them both. Most of the children and their parents would be dead, these memories lost in time forever. They threw out boxes of clothes, house goods, and expired food. It was three by the time both Max and doc had finished throwing out everything and stacking the rest they were keeping in individually labeled boxes. "I am beat, can we rest for a while?" "No, doc said. We must look at the space, plan, and start construction.

This will need to be done by tomorrow night at the latest. At five we can go get Sam. We can get her here before everyone else gets up. The men got started with planning. Each room would have a built-in bunk, a toilet, and a sink, and a light switch on the outside. The office will have a camera and be about ten by twelve feet. With Sam having her own secure space, the team would be safe if she shifted in her sleep. Both men decided to put the men's beds on one wall and a toilet/sink area in a small five by six-foot space. This will make it easier for them to clean up in the morning and use the restroom. Since the crew showers where on the other side of the ship.

By this time, Max decided they should go get Sam before the crew got up. When Max and doc reached the office, Sam was still in her panther form and asleep. They clicked on the intercom to the room and let her know it was time to get up. "Sam, we need you to get up, we have to move you. We are moving you to our new living space before everyone gets up". Sam slowly got up and realized she was still a panther. "You want me to move through the ship like this?" "Yes, if you stay in the shadows, just don't step under any lights. No one will be able to see you, you blend into the darkness around you. We will have a flashlight for us, and you just follow" Max said. "I hope you are right."

Sam reminded Max to get her some clothes after breakfast, she wanted to try and change back into herself for the day. She followed them through a small passageway she had never seen before. It continued to get darker, more mold was developed on the walls, and every breath she could feel the mold clinging to her lungs. They finally reached a door at the end of the hallway. It was yellow and had CARGO HOLD written in bold red letters. Max and doc opened the big door, motioning for her to go in. As she walked in, she could see a wide opening at the back of the room, which lead to the cargo door. She smelled the salty air rushing in, which was more welcoming than the moldy air from the walk down. Max closed the door before anyone could see her. Sam could see why Jack had chosen this space for her team. It was massive! She would have more privacy, could stay with her team, which she liked the most, and not to mention the cargo dock.

Having the cargo dock right here would help them get in and out of the ship for missions. They could enjoy the fresh air, sit, and watch the sunset. "We are going to build you a secure privet room in here, and the team will sleep against this wall. You will have a bathroom, and a camera for safety, monitoring the outer door. There will be a camera facing the men's bunks as well. "What do you think?" Doc asked. "It is big here! I love the open space and enjoy the sun on the deck. One thing I thought about was, won't others come in?" "No, only your team will have keys, no one else," doc answered. "We should get to work then!" "You can't do much in that form Sam, but we can start gathering materials, you can stay here" Max stated.

They left Sam in search of supplies. Max and doc did not know how they were going to find everything they needed, build it, and without telling anyone on the ship what it was for. Plus, not tell them what Sam had become. Over the next few days, the team had their new living space built and ready to live in. Sam watched them build from sun up to sundown. She would help carry the things she could, using her back as support. Doc and the team had made their rooms, without ever letting anyone know what they had been up to. Now, Sam could live here without any concerns. She did not need to worry about being seen or worry about harming others.

Max was beginning to be concerned for Sam though, she has been in her panther form for days now. She continues to try and change, trying to calm herself, but at night, she would dream of the dark ones and wake up like a panther again. There was no ending in sight. She and Max worried, she would never be able to shift back into her human self. Many days she spent time sleeping, relaxing on the dock, and imagining what it would feel like to be a panther forever. Would that be her future? Be a panther forever? Just like the wolves she had encountered on the mission.

Chapter 8

PANTHER

Sam enjoyed practicing her panther abilities, learning how to focus in on each one that she has discovered thus far. When Sam was on the loading dock, she could identify the boat location, they were somewhere by the equator, because of how hot, humid, and heavy the air was. Sam loved it when the mist from the waves would blowback on her face. Over time she began identifying stars. This would help her map their travels through the sea. Each night she would identify new star systems she had not learned in school. She would draw them using her nail on the loading dock floor. It did not take long before the deck was covered with different solar systems and its stars.

She would just sit and listen to the water hitting the haul, and crew members talking. The sound of passing whales where always her favorite, but she did notice some changes in the whale's echo. They were different then she remembered. Each whale the boat passed, created a distinct echo, they seemed to be warning the rest of the pod, the ship was coming their way. Sam would have never imagined, being this in tune with her surroundings and environment. Day after day, Sam stayed in her panther form. Doc had even tried to give her some relaxation medication, but just as she thought she was going to change, she fell back asleep and dreamt of the dark ones.

In her dreams she would be battling, winning the fight then out of nowhere she would be captured. Night after night, Sam wondered if her body was telling her what was to come of their future. She often thought she might be in this form forever. "What could I be doing wrong? I did it before, why is it not working now?" She would ask herself.

Many weeks had passed since Sam was in human form. Doc had recently ordered some new test, in the hope, there is a medical reason for her situation. Sam overheard Max and doc talking about how the bites she received, could have impacted her body. That means the panther is still trying to protect her. If the bits had stopped her from changing back. This means her body was trying to prevent the venom from killing her. The following day Max came to talk with her. "Sam doc has some news. He wants to give you a booster shot. It may or may not help your body heal. Or it could increase your panther strengths, he is unsure if it will harm you or make you better." "I'll try anything! But what if it makes me worse, what if I am a panther forever, no changing back?" "We just don't know, we can only hope for the best. What do you want to do Sam?" Max asked. Sam could not even imagine being a panther for the rest of her life, nor could she imagine changing into a dark one, or worse yet dying. Sam walked up to the doc and said, "I am in! I'm ready for my shot".

"Doc please leave once you give me the shot. I don't want to hurt you or anyone else if it goes badly". "Sam, you will not hurt us. We will back away from you slowly, and Oscar will tranquilize you if he has to." Sam walked into her room and braced herself for the upcoming shot. She calmed her breathing, told herself it will all be okay. As soon as doc stuck Sam, with the needle, Sam's panther kicked in and whipped doc with her tail. Facing them, she began to growl. Sam, of course, at this point didn't realize what she was doing. Every time she was hurt, she would lose herself within the panther. It was like she no longer existed, just blackness all around her. No conscious, no ability to talk, see, or think. Max jumped back and reacted to Sam's aggressive behavior towards doc. "What are you doing? We are here to help!" With no response, Max motioned to Oscar, and he shot her with a tranquilizer dart.

Sam awoke hours later with no memory of what happened and Max looking over her while she slept. "What happened Max?" "As doc stuck you, you turned to attack us, Oscar had to shoot you with a tranquilizer dart." "I sorry! Did I hurt him? That was what I was scared of". "You knocked doc over is all, just a few bumps and bruises. Nothing he could not fix. But Sam, the shot worked. You are now back to your human form". "WHAT! That is wonderful! Can I eat with everyone today then? dinner smells wonderful!" "Doc said not until your done with observation, it should be fine to go to breakfast tomorrow. You have only twelve hours left, that's nothing, you have been locked up in here for months, it seems." Max was right, what is one more day.

Sam struggled throughout the day. She was anxious about hanging out with her friends, whom she missed severely, and was worried about going back to sleep. Sam tried everything, working out, reading, cleaning, but nothing calmed her enough to sleep. Then sleep finely found her about one in the morning. Sam, of course, had to wake up early. Even before the six o'clock alarm. She was excited to find herself still human. She set up, got dressed, and ready for breakfast before her team was even awake. She found herself watching Max sleep.

Max's bunk was right under Oscar's. "Max," she said in a whispered tone, "are you up?" "No! Did I need to be? What time is it?" "About 530 in the morning." "Why are you up, we have another thirty minutes until we need to be up, go away." "No way! I must get out of here. I've been locked up forever it seems! Let's go". "Fine! But doc said one of us must go with you, at all times". "I would rather it be you, then someone else." "Were all up now, Sam!" said Oscar. "Sorry," Sam said in an impatient voice. She waited, anxiously for the men to get ready. Sam noticed her senses were more defined then what they had been. She could hear noise coming from Max, as he slid on his shirt, smell the overwhelming abundance of mold on the ship's walls, and even taste breakfast from the smell coming through the vents. Something was different this time, she could control her senses better than ever before. "Good, you already."

Sam lead the way through each corridor with ease, leaving her team behind running after her. "Sam slow down, please!" yelled Max. "Someone is going to notice us running after you, remember no extra attention! Nothing!" Oscar said. "Sorry guys I had no idea I was going that fast, what have you all told everyone about me? What do I tell everyone?" "We just told them, you were sick and under observation," Max said.

When Sam walked into the kitchen, she was welcomed back with open arms from all her friends. "Hey Sam, how are you feeling?" They said all in unison. "I am glad to be back and feeling better thanks for the asking." "You sound excited to be back," Nigel stated. "Yes, I really am glad, but I am famished, can we eat?" "Yes, of course!" they all said. Sam got in line for breakfast with her friends and team. She could smell the waffles, eggs, bacon, and syrup. It was making her mouth water. The smells were just as good as watching the sunrise in the morning. She filled her plate full. Alice was in aw when she saw Sam's overflowing plate. "I have never seen you eat this much Sam!" "Sorry I have been stuck eating rations for months. This smells, wonderful!" Right after Sam got her plate and sat down, she started eating.

Every bit tasted better than the one before. It was like Sam had never eaten before in her life. Every herb, every berry, had a more defined taste then what it had a month ago. In the excitement of eating, Sam did not notice that she was eating like an animal. When she looked up from her plate, the whole ship had been staring at her. Sam was so embarrassed, got up, and ran back to her room. Not even thinking about it, Sam ran as fast as she could, leaving the kitchen and everyone behind her. When she had made it back to her room, moments later, Max walked in. He rushed to hug her. She embraced his hug, holding him tight, and at that moment, she was finely able to take a breath.

His embrace, released all her stresses, made her feel safe and loved. "I don't want to go back, they were all looking at me like I was crazy. You could have told me that I was acting like that you know". "I was just as shocked as you! Sam" Sam looked up at him, looking deep into his eyes and felt an urge, to kiss him. She rubbed the bottom of his soft lips with her thumb, as he caressed, her cheek with the tips of his fingers. Her heart started beating faster, as he leaned in to kiss her. As their lips meet, it felt like heaven its self-had touched her. After a few minutes of an embrace, they were interrupted "There, you both are!" Scolded Oscar and Rex. "Stop that before your faces fall off." Max and Sam just started laughing. She had never felt this way about anyone before. This was all new to her, but she did not want to go too fast. Part of her longed for more, but the other part was glad Rex and Oscar came looking for them.

"Evelyn is looking for us all, we need to go meet with her, let's go you two" Oscar scolded again, finding their laughter not slightly funny. Sam and Max walked together, holding hands all the way to Evelyn's office. Holding hands distracted her from what might be waiting for them in Evelyn's office. When they reached her office, Sam could hear Jack's voice arguing with her about something, it was hard to make out. They reached the door and knocked, both Evelyn and Jack answered, "Come in! Thanks for joining us" "We have another mission we need you all to go on, and we need to go over our plans with you." Evelyn said. "In two days, you four will leave the boat in search of a hard drive that was stolen from us when the war broke out. It has information on it that could help us win the war against the dark ones". "Do you have any idea where it is? Or is this a search and find or die mission?" Sam inquired. "It was taken by the dark ones, and we believe it is in one of their main headquarters. The dark ones are more intelligent than we originally thought. They are not just driven to kill and multiply. They want to take over the world. If they open and use the information, they can find us and take us out; plus, others who are hiding from them as well" Evelyn stated. "What is on the hard drive?" Max asked. "It holds the blueprints to a surveillance system. The system can send up drones with cameras and weaponry. It will search, target all non-hybrid humans and kill them" Evelyn said. "Really? How do you know this?" Oscar asked. "I may run this ship, but I also work with other head leaders, who survived the main phase of the war. We have been working together to find and locate the hard drive. We would like to find it and use it to kill all the dark ones. We can take our lives back and win this war". "This is the first any of us are hearing about this. How can we trust that you are not sending us to die" Sam demanded, "Don't Speak to me that way! I have warned you about this before. I don't care if you don't trust me, Sam, you will follow my orders and do whatever you ordered to do".

Sam, Max, Oscar, and Rex said yes mam all at the same time. "I am also adding a new member to your team, Rose is an electronics specialist, who knows the system well." "We have not trained with her before, why?" Oscar asked. "She is an expert in programming, you will need her to test the hard drive." "Can't Nigel go with us then? He is better at programming. At least we know him and have worked with him before" Sam asked. "No, Rose is going!" Evelyn scolded. "Now you guys need to draft a plan and report back to me by tonight for approval. Here are the GPS coordinates, you may all leave my office now!"

Sam and the team left Evelyn's office, all frustrated and not wanting to go on this mission. None of them thought they would come back alive. "I can't believe that they have been keeping all this from us, and the crew, and who is this Rose woman? I just want to explode!" Sam yelled. "Sam, they are the boss, the leader of our ship. No matter if we agree with them or not, we have to follow orders." Oscar stated. "I am not in the military. I don't know how to follow blindly into battle like you do. I like to know why I am doing what I'm being asked to do". Sam argued back. Oscar and Sam glared at one another and continued walking to their room.

When they entered the cargo bay, Sam just exploded on Oscar. Telling him how she would never follow Evelyn.

Evelyn was not a good woman and was going to lead them right into the enemy's hands. Oscar reminded her that no matter what she said, she is a solder now. Which means Sam will complete this mission. She is not following Evelyn, but Oscar. He would never let harm come her way. They are a family now, nothing would change that. At that moment, Sam calmed down, took a deep breath, and was remembered that she is fighting the wrong person. She and the team took a moment to breath before they began to plan the mission.

"Since Oscar and Rex are the only ones, who have been in the military and lead many missions I vote that they plan the attack" Max stated. "Do you all concur?" "Sam said, I do but want to help plan it. That is the only way the rest of us will learn how to plan our own missions. If something were to happen to Oscar or Rex, I want to be able to think and act like a soldier." Oscar and Rex agreed that Oscar would continue to take the lead, for this mission and those to come. "Let's get started then," Oscar said.

Chapter 9

THE MISSION

"If the GPS coordinates are correct, we will need to use the speed boat, for a water excursion. We will come ashore about there (Oscar pointed to a location on a map), where the shore is the least exposed. We will be about 35 klicks away from headquarters. Now, we don't know what the layout is for their HQ, nor do we know how many dark ones will be there. Since there are so many unknowns here, we could be walking right into a trap," Oscar stated. "First thing, for the rest of us who have never been in the military, what the hell is a klick?" Sam inquired. "One klick equals one kilometer. It is about 22 miles away from our shore excursion point" Oscar said. "What will be the plan if we are overtaken by the dark ones? We need to plan for the worst. I can't take them all out," Sam said. "I really don't know Sam. We will just need to take the new ammunition, doc helped create. It will explode on impact, we will use less ammo this way. If everyone agrees, we can take this plan to Evelyn and get some sleep for tomorrow." "Yes! They all agreed".

Max and Sam decided to sleep in the same room to

make space for Rose. Rose joined them right after Oscar left. She was maybe six-foot, in her early twenties, and with copper-red hair. She was slimmer and taller than Sam expected, with deep blue eyes. "Hello everyone, I am Rose. I know none of us have worked together before but believe me when I say that I am excited about this mission with you all. Ready to kick some dark one's behinds". "You may be excited, but this is not just a walk in the park. The dark ones are dangerous, and it is dangerous for us to have an undisciplined programmer slowing us down," Rex scolded. "I am not undisciplined! Evelyn has been training me for months. I am ready for this, and I am not going anywhere. You guys better get used to that fact!" Rose stated. With nothing more said, Sam and Max, headed to bed, "Goodnight get some sleep." The next morning Sam was the first to awake. She nudged Max awake and proceeded to get the team-up. "Good morning everyone, it's 0230, and we need to get ready for the mission. "What? Why so early?" Rose asked. "We need to hit the shore and get to headquarters before daybreak" Oscar reported. Everyone quickly set up their gear, got breakfast, and then checked out their weapons and ammo.

Sam had a new backpack created for her. It would strap to her panther body and expand when she changed in and out of her human form. Sam also packed more clothes than her team. This way if she shifts into another form, then back out, she will have clothes to put back on. Oscar pulled Sam aside, "can you try and shift into panther form as soon as we hit the shore? We could use your senses before we run into any dark ones." "I can try, but I don't know how to control it very well yet." "So be it, but just try for me please?" Oscar asked. "I will do what I can Oscar." "Let's get the cargo hold open and, in the boat, time is not on our side. We will have a thirty-minute ride from the boat to the excursion point." Oscar said.

When the cargo door opened, Sam felt a rush of salty air hit her face. She could see the shore in the distance. The lights on in some of the buildings, but no one to be seen for miles. Sam followed behind Max as her team loaded the boat. "I want complete silence all the way there. Use the hand signals you have been practicing," Oscar said. The ride into shore felt ominous, something was wrong, but she could not figure out what quite yet. Sam imagined what the headquarters would look like, and how protected it would be. Would they really be successful at gaining entry, and finding the hard drive? She began thinking about her first change, the feeling, thoughts, surroundings, smells, and what she heard. She felt the inner animal rise within her. She slowly took a deep breath to remember where she was, and the feeling slowly passed. She could do this! Become a panther at will, all she needed was practice. The boat came to a stop a few miles from shore. "We swim here! The boat will be safer in the water". Oscar reminded. "Why is it safer for us to swim then to take the boat to shore?" Rose asked. "If you really knew about the dark ones you would know they do not like the water. Keeping the boat here will keep it safe from the dark ones. Let's stop talking and get into the water" he scolded.

The bay was ice cold. Sam was the first to enter. It took

her breath away, almost the same experience she had the first mission. It smelled like rotten seaweed. Sam could sense something in the water that would not be friendly. She motioned to her team, pointing into the water and about twenty feet from them. Whatever it was, it was fast, Sam could feel the current forcing its way towards them. She grabbed Max, Oscar, Rex, and Rose by their arms, and into the water. Sam exploded into a swim, pulling them behind her like a speed boat. The object in the water moved swiftly towards them, the faster she swam, the quicker it swam to catch up. Sam used all the energy Sam had, one stroke at a time, one last push, the shore was just a few feet away. When she thought they were safe, an object emerged from the water and grabbed Rose. It was something out of a Sci-Fi movie. Sam had never seen this kind of creature before. It looked like a giant crab with squid tentacles stretching out from it. The crab part of the beast was brick red. It was massive, the size of a whale. By the time they reached the beach, the crab had a tentacle around Rose's leg. It was to, late Sam had to make a choice, risk every team member's life or let the crab take Rose. Before Sam or anyone else could do anything, Rose was gone, along with the creature.

    With a gasp of air, Sam turned into a caracal. She had black-tipped ears, a white underbelly, with white circles around each eye and nose, with a brown/grey coat. Sam growled, at the rest of her team (as if to say let's go) and walked away. Sam did not realize that she shifted into a different cat, a caracal. Max, Oscar, and Rex were still laying on the beach. None of them could believe what just happened. Sam had saved them, but it was too late for Rose. None of the men knew how to wrap their minds around what had happened. At the same time, they could not stay there, they had a job to do. Each of them got to their feet and started pursuing Sam towards the main headquarters. Whispering to Sam, Max told her what she looked like and asked if she needed anything. "I just need the GPS for coordinates. There are some dark ones about five klicks away, if we are quiet, we can sneak around them and keep going without being noticed" she said. Max helped Sam, and on they went. Sam's new animal form provided her with different abilities and skills. She was lighter on her feet, faster, and seemed to have stronger senses. She led the team away from the dark ones and back up behind their position. The plan was to continue to headquarters' and find the hard drive. With Rose dead, the team did not know what they were looking for. Sam and the team were anxious but knew if they did not try Evelyn would have their lives. Sam continued to lead the team, one step at a time, around every corner, there was a dark one, the team had to either eliminate or sneak around.

Everything around them seemed foreign. The buildings were overgrown with green and brown mosses with vines. The streets were growing grass, which was encroaching on the sidewalks around them, street lights had toppled over, and most buildings were starting to topple over too. Sam continued through the streets of what she believed was New Jersey. Everything happening, Sam still could not believe where she was, or that she was leading a team of military men. Sam and the others had finally reached HQ (headquarters). There were dark ones everywhere guarding the doors, the windows, and the roof. "Oscar, what's the plan now?" Sam asked, in a hushed voice. "I don't know if there is a silent way to do this. Where outnumbered, and we don't even know if the hard drive is in the building. Do you have any ideas?" Asked Oscar. "I will go around the building and take out the lower level of the guards, while Rex gets up high and takes out the dark ones on the roof. Oscar; you and Max go into the building after I clear the front door, you two start looking for the hard drive, I will meet you inside." Sam said.

As the battle begins, Sam changed into her panther. The panther has the most robust bit of all cats, can hide in the dark, and was silent when walking. Sam could hide in the darkness and made her way to the front of the building. Sneaking up behind the dark ones was the natural part, but taking them out was more challenging. Sam had to bite their throats as hard as she could and swiftly. When Sam had reached the first dark one, Rex had begun his assault. Pop, pop, pop, is all Sam heard as she moved from one dark one to another, clearing the door for Max and Oscar. Sam was covered with blood from her first two attacks as Max and Oscar came up to her. She motioned them through the doors and reminded them to work fast, she would be back. As they entered the building, Sam continued her assault on the remaining dark ones. Every pop from the high-powered rifle, Sam knew that more dark ones would be heading straight for them, now that they were making so much noise. Each pop echoed off the buildings around them as if they were sitting in the Grand Canyon. It would be a homing beacon for them to follow, straight to Rex.

When Max and Oscar entered the building, they could see large pictures on the walls. The air conditioner was running, keeping the building overly cold. The men shivered as they walked down the hallway. They could smell a burst of air freshener, attempting to dissipate the overwhelming smell of death. The walls have begun to grow mold, so they were no longer white. Each step became more frightening, like they, were watching a scene from the movie Saw. There was dried blood on the floors and walls, human remains decaying throughout the first floor. There were no offices on this floor, and both Max and Oscar did not want to even start up the stairwell until Sam was there to go first. Sam must have heard their thoughts because right as they were heading towards the stairs, she came in behind them. Both men jumped with fright when she swept past them. "Come on guys let's get this done, Rex is running out of ammo, and maybe caught before we're done Sam reminded them."

Once they were in the stairwell, and before they could do anything, the doors closed, and gas grenades dropped from above. All three fought to open the doors while gasping for fresh air, they fell asleep. When the team awoke, they had no idea where they were, or how long they had been sleeping. Sam called out, "Are you guys up? Are you hurt?" Sam was still in panther form and could only make out their shapes, not if they were hurt. She could hear their hearts pumping, at least they were not dead. "We're fine, just tired" she heard them all say in unison "do any of you have your weapons or packs?" Sam inquired "No, whoever gassed us must have taken them, and tossed us in here. Where ever that is," replied Oscar. "I wonder what they're going to do with us?" Sam asked. "Who knows! Whoever they are, they are not going to be friendly. Make sure none of you talk to them about our lives or the White Cloud," said Oscar.

Suddenly, the light turned on, and the door opened. It took a minute for Sam's eyes to adjust to the bright lite. The room was painted with an off grey color, a table was in the middle, it looked like an interrogation room that Sam remembers seeing on TV shows. There were no windows and no other doors. Sam could not think of any other way of escape but through the main entrance. Even if Sam could fight their way out, she did not know what she was fighting her way into. Sam was concerned about her team and had no idea how to get them out of this one.

The floor was concrete with a drain in the middle. With that being said, Sam knew they were probably in the basement or on the main floor of the building. "Good morning, glad to see you all awake. Who might you all be" asked a man with a deep voice? "I'm Sam, that is Max, Rex, and Oscar. What will you do with us?" The tall man walked into view. He had long black hair, pale white skin, with black eyes. He was six-feet tall and had what looked like bit marks up and down on his arms. "You and your friends killed many of our soldiers, that took some skill. Sam, you are not a panther or human? Are you? Where did you come from?" The man asked. "We came from a town not far from here, we have been hiding out and training," Oscar stated. "There is no way that is true, but you can tell us what you will. We only want to gather some information from you, and let you go". "There is no way you are letting us just walk away, so let's cut to the chase shall we" Rex replied. "All right then! We want to per-sway you to come to our side" the man stated. "What makes you think we would ever do that?" Asked Sam "Once you hear what I have to say, if your answer is still no, then we will change your team, and you all can go. If you choose to stay, we will let them be". "It will not matter but go ahead," Oscar said. "Do anyone of you know what was happening in the government before the gas bombs fell from the sky?" "What do you mean," the team asked. "What was happening in the government and around the world?" "No," they said in unison. "All the world's leaders decided to work together for once. They wanted to lower the world's population, decrease our carbon footprint, and give the world a new start. We believe that the gas bombing and this war were their way of fixing our overpopulated world. Some individuals who are changed, keep their memories, their wits and all their emotions. Where others turn into deadly weapons. The world leaders picked a group of lab techs to create the gas used for the bombs, hoping it would kill half the world's population, not change everyone. They did not realize people would evolve into monsters or other creatures.

The head lab tech's name was Evelyn, we're not sure where she is or what has become of her, but we felt you all were her plan B." "Evelyn, you say?" Asked Sam. "Yes" "Can my team and I have a moment alone? Truly alone?" Sam asked. "Yes, we will give you some time to talk about our offers." Sam was angry enough to rip through all these dark ones and to make her way to the white cloud. She wondered though if this could be a trap. "Can we really believe him?" Asked Oscar. "I think we can. Why would they lie about this? What would they gain?"

"Sam, I know you don't like her, but take a step back and think about it all with a level head, not an emotional one," Oscar stated. "What do Rex and Max think?" she asked. "We are with Oscar, Sam. We need to see proof before we just believe them!" "Why don't we ask if they have proof. If she is what they say, then we take her out and if they don't have proof, am I supposed to let you three change or die?" Sam's voice cracked at the thought of losing any of them. "We can live with that Sam, it is our choice, and if we die or change then so be it." Oscar replied. Sam wanted to sway them, from their decision, but she knew it was a futile task. She kept her thoughts to herself and headed to the door, knocked, and waited for their response. She knew if they were anything like her, they could hear that knock from anywhere. Sam and the team did not wait long before the same dark one came back into the room. "I take it you all have made a decision?" "We would like to know what proof you have before we make a decision. We will not decide based on just your word alone," Sam said. "We have a video that was confiscated a few months ago. It is on a hard drive, I believe you all were looking for it. Let me talk to the leadership and be back with you. They may not want to show it to you. While you wait, I'll have some food brought for you".

"I am even more pissed off now! They have the hard drive, we risked our lives looking for. It seems we have been deceived! Evelyn wanted us to clean up her mess and risk our lives in the process," Sam yelled. The team sat in silence while waiting for food. Minutes later, two dark ones brought in four MRE's, with some water for the team to eat and drink. The dark female one was about 5'11, had dark red hair, gray eyes, and white skin. She was beautiful, not scary like the other dark ones. She was wearing a full black jumpsuit with combat boots, looked like something out of a comic book. Almost looked like a superhero, stiff, and ready to jump into action. The man had dark blue/gray hair, skinny body frame, red eyes, and white skin. He was shorter than the woman. He too wore black cloths, except he was wearing pants and a shirt, with his combat boots. Sam thanked them for the food as they left the room. Neither of them spoke a word, to Sam or the team. Just walked in, set down the food, and walk out. Like robots being controlled from another room. Neither had an expression or showed emotions either.

"How is everyone feeling?" Max asked. "I think we're all pretty wiped out. Why don't you three get some shut-eye, I'll stand watch" Rex said. It was not long after Rex volunteered to stand to watch that Sam and Max had laid down together and fallen asleep. Sam dreamed about the dark ones, and what he said about life before the war. She dreamed about her father "Sam life is changing, and there is nothing any of us can do to change that" is something her dad started saying before the bombs fell. Could this be what he was talking about? She drifted back to a few days before the war. She wished she could reach out and touch her mother's face again or fight with her brother. She was reliving her life. She remembered watching the news with her family. That happened often, her parents wanted them to be educated on what was happening around the world. The news story that day was about the world summit. It was planned to adjourn, in a few days. CNN shared who was planning to attend. Right, when she was beginning to remember what was reported, Sam was awoken by the door opening, and the male dark one entering the room. "My superiors have made the decision to let you watch the video. Take a few minutes to wake up and knock on the door when you are ready." Sam was relieved to hear the news but frustrated at being woke up when she was so close to remembering more about the world summit. She was hoping that the dream would show her what had happened at that summit.

As they began to wake up, the team thanked Rex for letting them rest. Oscar was just waking up when Sam asked if they were ready to watch the video because she was eager too! "Yes, have them come back in. Ask what time it is and what day, while we're at it," Oscar said. Sam knocked on the door, moments later the same dark one came in with a computer. "Okay, I'm keeping my word, here is the video. Let me know when you are done, I'll come back in," he said. Sam took a moment to ask what day it was and time. None of them could believe it had been three days since they had left the White Cloud. Sam and the team positioned themselves around the table where the video could be seen by them all. Sam pressed play; the footage of Evelyn began. Evelyn was in a lab with a few other men and women, the team did not recognize. "We have to get this right; one mistake and it will be over for us. This task was given to us, because we are the best in bio-genetic scientist, and on chemical warfare. They are counting on us to do this right. Remember we are doing this for our families. They promised us they would keep our families safe" Evelyn reminded the other lab techs. One of the lab techs, said, "this doesn't seem right! What if something goes wrong?" "It won't! Just do your job and save your families" Evelyn scolded. The video ended shortly after.

The lab was filled with lab rats and other animals. They had to be using them for tests. It was a small space, white walls, and a lot of equipment, and most of the equipment the team did not recognize. "Do you all believe him now?" Max asked. "It could be fake!" Oscar pointed out. "You just really don't want to believe! You have been taught for many years that the dark ones were the enemy. Evelyn is the enemy, and we need to do something about it," Sam scolded. "What are we to do Sam? Go confront her and be killed?" Rex said.

"It's not like we can go home and just shoot her! We need a plan. I'm not saying I don't believe the dark ones, but we need a plan". Oscar said. With that said, the dark one walks into their room "What do you think? Will you believe us now?" He asked. "We don't know what to believe. What do you think we can do?" Oscar asked. "We want you to join our team, train our men, and fight with us. We are aware that you know who Evelyn is! But are willing to work with you and keep you all alive" the dark one promised. "What you are saying is if we help you, we live?" They asked. "Yes, that is correct." "Can we have some time to talk again, please" Oscar asked. "Yes," The man again left the room.

Sam, Max, Oscar, and Rex gathered up to talk about the situation as quietly as they could. "You all know that if we do this, we all become spy's right?" Oscar asked. "Yes, but I don't see any other options. I cannot fight them all, and I don't want to see any of you taken and turned," Sam whispered. "She is right, Oscar, there is no military way out of this. We trust our captors and find our way out of this. At some point soon, we must return. It's been three days; Jack will know something is wrong if we're not back by tonight." Rex stated. "The plan will be to agree with their terms, a spy for them, and then what?" Max asked. "We won't know until this plays out. There are too many unknowns here," Oscar said. "Call them back in, Sam." Sam walked and knocked on the door. "Have you made a decision?" The dark one asked. "Yes, we will agree to your terms" Sam replied. "Great! I am Isaac and I am the captain of the army. I'll show you around, and we will get to know one another. Sam, what happened to you? You are different than our shifters". "I was given a serum and can change in and out of different cat forms. I cannot always control it, though" Sam replied. "We will change that you are extraordinary!" Isaac said.

Max felt jealous of how much attention Isaac was giving

Sam, he reached down and brushed her ear. She didn't notice, but Isaac saw the interaction and put his nose down to it. Like he was unimpressed by Max's behavior. As they continued down the hallway, Sam noticed the decor, smell, and lighting all began to change. Walls had fresh paint, pictures were new and interesting, it was like the foul odor, and human remains were meant to scare people away. They walked through the whole floor, to the stairwell, and up the two flights. When they walked through the next open door, Sam could see sleeping quarters.

The bunks were stacked three high and evenly on the walls. There had to be fifty or more, how could the wall hold them all up, Sam wondered to herself. Isaac showed the team to their bunks. Where the lockers were, and the supply closet. Isaac walked them into another big room. It housed a large kitchen and eating area. Then showed them into the unisex shower and bathroom. "Is this the only restroom and shower?" Sam asked. "Yes, there is a sign-up sheet on the outside of the bathroom. Men and women are to shower separately unless they are a couple. This way, everyone can shower privately and have their own space if they so choose.

Why don't you guys get cleaned up and I will be back to pick you up and take you to meet my superiors in about thirty minutes" Isaac stated. They all looked at each other, with blank expressions. None of them want to volunteer to shower first. Sam spoke up, "Should we get started. Maybe I clean up first since I'm a panther form?" "Sam, why don't you try to shift before we go up," Max asked. "I'll try to give me some time, and if I can't, then I'll let you guys get cleaned up." Sam stepped into the bathroom. She was unsure and did not know if she could change back into her human self. Sam was no longer who she once was; she is immune, with abilities to shift into different cat species. Maybe that was the missing key, she kept trying to change into who she was when her dad left her on the White Cloud. Instead of trying to turn back into who she has become. Sam began to feel her body change. She shifted from her panther into herself again. She pulled herself up off the floor and begin to take her shower.

It was strange being back on two legs. Sam had been shifted for three days now in the more time she spends as a panther, the less she remembers about her human self. It felt relaxing to have the water hitting her head and dripping down her body. She felt comfort in knowing that they were safe. At least safe for the moment. What was going to happen after they met Isaac's superiors? Sam focused her attention back on her shower and this bathroom. The bathroom was not very big, had brown tiles with a snow-white sink and toilet.

By the time, Sam was finished with her shower, the entire bathroom had filled up with steam. It was like the room was filled with an eerie fog. Sam felt as if somebody was watching her. She had an ominous feeling lingering around her. The hair on the back of her neck was sticking up, from her head down to her feet. She turned around, and there standing before her was Isaac. "What are you doing in here?" She yelled. "Just had to see it for myself, what a fine specimen," he said. "Excuse me! What gives you the right, to invade my space like this?" Sam scolded. "You're under our care Sam, and that's what gives me the right," "No! It does, not Isaac now please leave". "I'll leave, but you will be running back to me when your human "man" doesn't want to be with a shifter anymore." Isaac said as he left the restroom. He left it at that and walked away. Sam quickly got dried off and dressed. She felt her anger boiling inside her, rushing to the surface. Sam knew if she did not control it, she was going to shift. Sam took some deep breaths, and it helped her remember who she was. She decided to keep this incident to herself. Telling her team will only make them angry and possibly wreck their chances of getting home safe.

As she stepped out of the bathroom, there stood Isaac, again waiting for her. "Where is my team?" "They are in the mess hall, I thought I would wait for you, Sam." "Please stop! Just like someone else please Isaac". "No, we should go to eat Sam. Then I'll take you and them to my superiors". "Fine!" Sam followed Isaac into the mess hall where she found the team. "Who is next for the shower? You guys should hurry!" Sam stated. "We will just go do it at once, we're used to it anyway," Oscar said with a laugh. Sam again was left with Isaac. "What do you really want with me Isaac?" "I want you! Nothing that you can do about it really. There will be a time when you will come asking me to be with you, protect you, and care for you. I'll be here waiting," Isaac said. "Well, I'm not going to be coming your way, buddy!" Isaac just smiled. He did not give away any facts or tell her how he knew this. He just walked away, like a robot.

Sam continued to eat what was supposed to be biscuits with gravy. It looked like thick bread, with brown sauce. The dressing looked almost like mud, and it tasted like Charcoal. Sam felt that Isaac was holding something back from her. He was mysterious and did not know anything about boundaries. When Sam had finished, she put her plate away and walk out to meet Isaac and the guys. In addition to that, he was the same Red-headed dark one. The one who helped feed them during the interrogation. "My name is Red. I'm here to walk with you all". She must have been from the south she had a broad southern accent. "Nice to meet you. I am Sam". When the team was done showering, they met Sam, Isaac, and Red, by the bunks. "Let's go! time is wasting," Sam said. "This is Red; she is walking with us." Isaac led the way, he walked them up to three more flights of stairs. By the time they reach the correct floor, Max, Rex, and Oscar were out of breath, trying to keep up with Red, Sam, and Isaac. "When we enter the office, I will introduce you. Do not speak unless asked direct questions," Isaac said.

Chapter 10

THE PLAN

Isaac walked the team into the office, it had white walls, with a big window facing the bay. The room had a long table, with five chairs and five dark ones sitting upon them. The board was made up of two women and three men. Isaac began introducing them " the older woman to the left is Robin, next to her is Danika, the first man is Ian, then you have Aaron and Jon. This is Sam, Max, Oscar, and Rex." Robin was of a heavier build, shorter than the others, red hair, blue eyes, with pale white skin. She must have been a biker in her human life since she had many old and fading tattoos. She was in her late fifties and had a permanent scowl on her face. Danika was also short, and of medium build. She had pointy ears, electric blue hair, one brown eye, and one green eye. She was in her early twenties and seemed to use sarcasm in her responses to others. Ian was a tall man in his thirties. He had black eyes, brown hair, and white skin. He did have cuts across his exposed chest, looked deep and made from some kind of knife. Arron and Jon could be twins. Both had the same orange hair, red eyes, and pale white skin.

They too looked to be in their thirties, with pointed ears, extending past the top of the skull.

"It is nice to finally meet you all. If you all could have a seat we can get started," Robin said. "We understand that you are nervous to be meeting with us and discussing a truce or a Cease-fire, so to speak, under these circumstances. We are the enemy, after all. Some of us, when we are bitten, change into what we call maladies. You have others who turn into a hybrid-humans, and lastly, a small amount of us have taken animal forms, like you Sam. We call them the shifters. We have been looking into what happened and who dropped the gas bombs. The United Nations (NATO) worked with other world leaders. NATO is the mastermind behind the bombs. The intent was to lower the world population. The belief was if the world continued to grow at the rate it was, the planet would have died, and all-natural resources would have been depleted. This was the only way they saw fit to do the damage quickly and with minimal suffering.

What they didn't plan was for was Evelyn and others in places of power to change the chemical makeup of the bombs. We want to take back the control, destroy the maladies, and human leaders who created this mess," Robin stated. "What do you need us to do for you?" Asked Oscar. "We want Sam to stay here with one of you. She will work with us to control her powers and start hunting and destroying the maladies. Then, the other two go back home. Report to Evelyn that Sam and whomever else stay behind have died. Lastly, whoever goes back would need to be our spies to help destroy Evelyn," Ian said. "That is something we have to discuss with one another. Whoever returns, would be taking a great risk. How would they report information back to Sam and Isaac?" Oscar Asked. "Since the world turned inside out, there are no more cell phones or other modern electronic communication. We normally use old, handheld radios from the world war era. There only effective for a few miles and you live too far away for that. We will need to devise another plan. We do have shifters who can become invisible to your kind and report information back to us," Ian said. "Can we have an hour or so to discuss this amongst ourselves?" Oscar Asked. "Yes, we'll be waiting," Aaron said.

Sam and her team were escorted to a different conference room. "I say we do this. I believe them, after seeing the video, but I don't want them to know where the White Cloud is located. How can someone be a spy without giving the position away? We also need to create another plan. One that would bypass any side agendas the dark ones may have. I don't want any of our friends or family on the White Cloud getting hurt," Sam said. "Well, I am not leaving Sam!" Max said. "I don't think it should be you with her. There will be allies on the ship who will only hear the news from you. I say Rex stays with Sam. He has military experience just like I do. He could be good for her, train the dark ones, and keep an eye out for Sam. Sorry Max, your feelings for her cannot control our choices" Oscar stated. "No way, I don't care if your right. I only do this under protest," Max said. "Their right, Max, we have to be smart here, and not underestimate the dark ones" Sam replied. "Are we doing this? Sam and Rex stay behind, and Max and I go back to base? We have to make a good cover story and need to go back injured". Oscar said. "So, not only do I lose Sam, but need to be injured in the process. Great, just great!" Max stated with irritation in his voice. "There is no other way, Max. This must work. We will be together again!" Stated Sam. "What is our cover story?" Max inquired. "Why don't you guys report that while we were trying to take headquarters Rex and I died in the attack, and due to your injuries, you headed home. This way, the truth is not too far off from the lie," Sam said. "I like that idea they will not suspect anything different. How do we keep others safe and still spy on Evelyn at the same time?" Max Asked.

"The dark ones said they had a plan for that, let's see what they have in place, but if it gives up our location, I don't want to do it," Rex said. They walked back to the office, where the dark ones were waiting for them. "We have decided to work with you. Sam and Rex will stay behind, and Max and I will go back. We will need a few injuries and some ripped clothes. We also want to hear more about how you plan on us reporting information. We do not want to give away our position," Oscar said. "You guys are very wise! We already tracked your movements before you attacked us. We know where your base is. We do not plan to hurt anyone but leadership who did this to our families and yours!" Jon said. "There is no need to hide it from us. We plan to have you take a shifter with you. She shifts into a bird. She will not hurt anyone and can fly back and forth to us with information," Robin said. "Why not tell us sooner?" Max Asked.

"We wanted you all to feel safe, and understand we were not holding your friends over your heads to force you to be corporate," Jon said. "Thank you for not doing that! We need to get ready and plan our return. We have all agreed to this and hope for everyone's sake, Evelyn does not catch on. She will kill us all!" Oscar said.

Chapter 11

RETURNING HOME

Sam was uneasy! She didn't know if she could trust the dark ones. Sam was worried about Max and the rest of her friends. Her friends would grieve for her, and think she was dead. Will they ever forgive, once they knew the truth? She wouldn't know those answers until they came to live with her after the final war. She had to keep herself and Rex alive, not focus on Max, her friends, or the life she would be leaving behind. In time they all would be together again.

Sam, Max, Oscar, and Rex walked together back down to their bunks. "We are still doing this? When do we leave?" Max asked. "We need to go now! Before anyone on the White Cloud gets Suspiciousness. It will take us a little longer to get back. We will be injured, and hopefully, the shifter can change into a bird; large enough to carry us one at a time to our boat. Being hurt in that water is not something that is on my bucket list," Oscar stated. Just then, Isaac walked in with a young woman "this is

Chloe, she will be going with you." Chloe was a small, 15-year-old girl, maybe. She has lime green hair with deep blue eyes. "Hi, everyone what can I do to help?"

"It depends on what birds you can shift into!" Said Oscar. "I can shift into any bird. I am good at switching into hawks, eagles, and an ostrich." "Can you carry us one at a time to our speed boat?" Oscar asked her. "I can try! How far is the shore to the boat, Oscar?" "It is 15-20 klicks. We have no way of knowing if it has moved, over the last three days," Oscar said. "The tide has not been low in the last three days. It probably hasn't moved much. I think I can carry you both one at a time. It will be close," Chloe said.

"Who is doing the damage? I want to get the pain done and over with" Max said "Who would you prefer" Isaac Asked. "I think I would like Oscar and me to fight," Max said. "I agree with Max," Oscar stated. Isaac showed them to the training room, where the men's packs were waiting for them. Oscar and Max slid into the ring and began to box. Oscar got in a few punches to Max's face and jaw, and one to his kidneys. Max spat out thick red blood on the mat. Max then, was able to hit Oscar in his torso, doing severe damage to his stomach, ribs, and kidneys. Isaac also recommended they take some knife wounds. Max was hit by Isaac's throwing knife on his lower leg as he maneuvered to miss the throw. Then, one hit Oscar, it landed in his forearm. "Dang! Isaac, you could have warned us! Those knives hurt," Oscar yelled. Within fifteen minutes, both men looked like they had been through a few ruff fights. Brushes and welts began to show up, and both knife wounds where wrapped, to prevent germs, during the trip back to the white cloud.

Sam and Max walked down to the lobby together. "I am going to miss you! It feels like my heart is being ripped out of my chest. I don't want you to go even though it needs to happen," Sam said. "I know Sam, I will miss you. I hope you stay safe and wait for me. There will be a time when we can be together again," he said. Max reached out to embrace her with a hug. She felt like the world was taking away her only soul mate. Sam began to cry, knowing it might be the last time they saw each other. She then reached up and kissed him ever so lightly on how cheek and walked away. As Sam walked away, crying, Max and Oscar made their way down to the beach, along with Chloe. She flew overhead five feet or so above them. It took them about 45 minutes to an hour to make it to the beach, with all their injuries. On their way back, Max and Oscar discussed in more detail, what they were going to say to Jack and Evelyn. "I hope this is the right thing to do," Max said. "It was our only move! We have to do this. We can only do our best. This just happens to be our best. Sam will be okay! She has Rex, and he will protect her." Oscar stated. "We need to stick to the same or similar stories. If they are the same, Jack will know something is wrong," Max said. "Well, we can tell them everything that happened, up to HQ, when everything changed. At that point in the story, we can make up our own versions. We were separated, and lost Rex and Sam," Oscar said. "It better be, convincing! That's all I got to say. Jack will smell a rat. Sam is a weapon to them now, and her abilities are only getting stronger. That was my only mission, to keep her at my side, and protect her, their weapon. I can't believe this is all happening this way. Jack is going to kill me," Max said. "Shut up! Chloe might be able to hear you, dang Max."

Once there, they could still see the boat floating about. I had moved out only a few feet. Chloe took a test flight out and back. She wanted to test the distance while in flight. "Okay, showtime Chloe. What bird will you be shifting into?" Oscar Asked. Chloe suddenly shifted into a Marital Eagle. Her wingspan had to of been more than eight feet wide. She had brown and black feathers from head to tail, with a white underbelly. "I will grab you one at a time, from your packs. I don't want to hurt either of you so stay still?"

"We can handle it, let's get going," Oscar said. She flew up into the sky, then suddenly, Oscar was gone. It startled Max, he did not even hear her grab him. Max was just glad that she was on their side. Max kept an eye out for Chloe. He was expecting her this time. She swooped down, and one-minute later, he was next to Oscar. Chloe flew both men to the boat, within five minutes, it seemed. Chloe landed back down, next to the men as a Peregrine Falcon. She was lightweight, black and white, with her same deep blue eyes. Her eyes reminded Max of his best friend back when the world was not at war. His friend's name was Kryen, and she used to play with him every day. They were neighbors and were in the same grade all the way through school. He often wondered about her if she was alive or dead. Even worse was she a dark one. Max was brought out of his daydreaming by the roar of the boat engine. They were off to the white cloud, without Sam and Rex, worse yet they had to pretend they were dead.

For Max, that would be easier, Sam was like dead, he did not know if he was ever going to see her again. Max and Oscar discussed their plan and how they would get Chloe messages in and out of the white cloud. "Chloe you will need to turn into a pigeon, we have plenty of them on the ship, all the time. That will make it easier for you to move about. At night you can sleep in Sam's room, once we disable the cameras. With her being gone, they won't need them on. There are cameras everywhere, you will need to be very careful not to talk with us outside our room. If your caught, you would be tortured or worse killed," Oscar said. "I understand! What happens if the camera does not get turned off and removed?" "With Max being the head of security, he will have the chance to go meet you on the main deck when he wants, there are no cameras up there" Oscar replied.

As they approached, the White Cloud Chloe flew a short distance away, maintaining visual on the ship and men. Awaiting the signal to load the cargo hold. They could hear the boats look out whistle signal "someone approaches." Max and Oscar took the boat towards the cargo bay. With grim faces and ready for action, Evelyn and Jack met them at the dock. Evelyn and Jack were excited to see them until they saw only Max and Oscar had returned. "Where are the others? Are you two hurt?" Jack asked. "They are all dead, and we almost did not make it back ourselves," Oscar stated. Evelyn and Jacks' faces changed from happy to horror. "What happened," Evelyn Asked. "Let them get seen by doc before you start questioning them, have you no heart? They lost their friends!" Jack yelled. Once you both have taken a shower, changed, and eaten, please come find me. We will talk then, there will be fewer ears around. "Yes, sir," both men said.

Chapter 12
THE DARK ONES

Sam walked back into HQ crying as Max walked away from her, not knowing when she will see him again. Red came up behind her, "he will be okay! And come back for you". "Thanks for the kind words, but I'm not so naïve to think that he is coming back for me, unhurt or even the same man he left as. Chances are that he will not be back and possibly die," Sam said sobbing. As the sunset, Sam decided to walk about the vast compound. Red had offered to show her around. "I've been here for a long time now. Shortly after the gas dropped, I changed. My family did as well but into maladies. I was alone and searching for safety and a new life. That's when Isaac found me, almost starved to death, skin, and bones. He and I became good friends right off the bat. I know he is ruff around the edges, but he has been good to me. You should give him a chance!"

"When he treats me like a person, human being, I might cut him a break. Right now, I just need to do something to take my mind off things" Sam said. "I'll give you that he does seem to like you. Isaac has wanted to meet you, since your first appearance a few months back. He was an observer, when you took out like those men, all by yourself" Red replied. "He was there? Red, that was my first shift, I was more animal then hybrid. It was a hard day, and a few months. I was not able to shift back into human form." "Isaac will be able to help you with that. He taught Chloe and me how to control our shifting. It is his superpower! Do you want to go eat dinner and sleep for a while?" Red asked. "Sure, let's eat, then I will head to bed for now."

Sam and Red walked together to the kitchen. Sam ate a Hamburger and fries. It was her first since she had left home. It smelled delicious; her mouth started watering before Sam even took a bite. Sam savored every bit, she was so fixed on eating that she did not notice the new on comers watching over her. She was nervous to ask where the burger meat came from. It did not taste like beef, but who knows what else it could be.

When she looked up from eating, ten dark ones were gazing at her. They were eager to meet the one shifter who still looked human. Many of them all looked the same. The same dark hair and eyes, with white skin, but there were a few who stuck out to her like Red and Chloe. "Sam let me introduce you to a few friends of mine, and I guess to the crowed collecting around us! Everyone this is Sam, she will be living with us and helping us fight the malady. Say a few words, Sam!" "I am Sam, I am 19, was given a serum to create a stronger human to fight you all, who we call the dark ones. I am looking forward to learning how to shift and start kicking some malady butts."

Red pushed the crowd back and introduced Sam to a few of her friends. They too stood out from the others. Sam this is Vixen, she has been a part of this group for a few months now. She can shift into almost every kind of dog" Red said. Vixen was a tall woman in her twenties, with blond hair and deep green eyes. She introduces herself, and Red continued. "This is Maximilian, he has been here since I have. He was found in the Seattle area after his family had changed into maladies. He can change into bears, any kind of bear, it is quite amazing Sam." Maximilian was a red-haired, yellow-eyed man in his mid-thirties. He too introduced himself to Sam. Red then introduced Sam to the last shifter at headquarters, "this is Jasmine, she is the youngest here. She does not remember much from her life since she was so young when she changed. Jasmine can change into bugs and is a spy for us most of the time." Jasmine is a five-foot-nothing kid. She had blond hair and red eyes. Her eyes were blood-red, Jasmine looked like a demon. Sam was perplexed, uncertain if she could become friends with any of the dark ones, who stood before her. Jasmine's name reminded Sam of Max. His sister's name was Jasmine. Could this be her? Sam did not want to pry, she would ask her about her life, and who knows if she will remember anyways.

Sam and the shifters sat and ate dinner together. She learned a tremendous amount of information about the dark ones and maladies. When they change into a dark one, it takes but a few minutes. You can see the change right away, and all it takes is just one bite. Maximilian told Sam that his parents changed right in front of him, then changed him, when he couldn't escape. Their unlucky, both his parents turned into a malady. Sam couldn't imagine how terrified he and the others must have been. She knew what was going to happen and was asleep, it was still scary when she awoke. Their change had to be ten times worse than Sam's. Sam learned that there is only one gene split that determines if you change into a dark one or a malady. The dark ones have been doing studies to try and reverse the effects of bites and gas. They have not been successful.

By the time they were done eating, Red had shown Sam to her bunk. "If you change in your sleep just lay on the bunk, until Isaac can start the training in the morning. He will teach you how to shift at will into all our cat shifts." "I am looking forward to that! I am excited to know what all I can do, and for once be able to control it, my shifting Red".

Chapter 13

BEGINNING

Sam woke up the next morning feeling rejuvenated. She was ready to learn more about herself and shifting. After, Sam had gotten prepared for the day she met Isaac by the kitchen. "Hello, Isaac! When do we start training?" "Now if you are ready!" "Show me the way" Sam said. She followed Isaac to the training room. It had a vast array of training equipment, red matted flooring, limited lighting, and a boxing ring in the middle of the room. "We should start by identifying what triggers your animal shifts, Sam. I want you to get into the ring with sparring gloves on. To see if physical fighting brings out your panther form". Sam followed his instructions and got into the boxing ring. She has wanted to kick his butt since he walked in on her, in the shower. She watched as he approached the ring. His hair was slicked back today, Sam felt an attraction for Isaac, just for a moment. He was more attractive then she had noticed before.

He was wearing a tight pair of shorts with a white tank top. His muscles bulged out, across his shoulders, and down his arms. Sam raised her fist as Max had taught her. Isaac swung at her first. She parried his swing and caught him in the ribs. "Don't treat me like I am a china doll, Isaac!" "As you wish Sam." Isaac punched back with speed and force. She could only parry one punch. Sam took the other blow to her stomach and hunched over, gasping for air. It felt like all the air in her lungs where gone, and she had to fight to breathe again. He again attempted to come down on her with a kick. Sam swept his leg from under him, and he landed on the ground beside her. Both stood up within seconds of one another. Sam came in with a roundhouse kick to his chest and knocked him over again. With a thud, he hit the floor. He began to stand, and Sam got him back. Another kick to his gut. "You are good Sam, who taught you?" He said with a labored breath. "Max did," she responded in a horsed voice.

"This is not brining, out you shift. There must be another trigger. When you shifted before, what started it? An action, smell, or feeling?" "I was walking with my team, when I felt a strange feeling, fear, I think. I began to feel hot, then just pain. I was one minute a human and the next a panther. I then, struggled to shift back into myself, Isaac." "You must not fear me! I will trigger that fear then!" He said as he got up. The next thing Sam saw was a group of dark ones entering the training room. All varying in size. They began to run at her with great force, creating similar fear in her, as she felt the first day she shifted. With the same result. She changed from her human form to her panther. Sam growled at the approaching dark ones. They stopped looking down at her with surprise. Sam looked at them, teeth showing, and began to walk towards them, with anger in her eyes. Isaac stepped in front of them, "Sam, what are you doing? They are not the enemy here." He ushered the group of men back and out of the room. "Come on, Sam, it's me, Isaac, remember?" Sam shifted her eyes back to Isaac, "I see you, I wanted to scare them out of here. Next time they will think twice about rushing me like that, you too Isaac."

"Okay, then! Now that we know fear will change you into your panther, we can begin to work together on changing, you into all other forms. Now change back into hybrid form, Sam." "I don't know how! Isaac, that's the problem. I was in my panther form for over a month's last time." "I am going to help you, Sam, we can do it together." Isaac bent down and looked her straight in the eyes. He reached his hand up to her face and gently rubbed her cheek. Sam felt a rush of emotion, it moved from her face through her body, until she was laying there looking up at Isaac. "All it takes Sam, is for you to think of something that removes your anger and replaces it with a different emotion. Here is a towel, get dressed".

Sam got up with the towel around her and walked into the bathroom. She felt ashamed, how could Isaac make her think in such a way? She did not like him, she hated him really. Nevertheless, he had gotten to her. Sam found a cupboard, full of spare clothes and put a set on. They were just a plain black shirt and pants. "Isaac this sort of thing must happen a lot. Is that why there is a cupboard of clothes in there?' "Yes, we all train here and get tired of destroying our own clothes." "I understand that one! I have ruined four or more outfits now" Sam said.

"The more you learn, the more cloths you will destroy. We should take a break and have some lunch. I want to take you out, show you where and how the maladies stay hidden." "That sounds more fun then, kicking your butt all day, Isaac" Sam, an Isaac, went back upstairs to the kitchen. She continued to eat hamburgers, it reminds her of her family and takes her mind there instead of in the present moment eating with Isaac. "Sam, how did you get to become a shifter? I know you have said it before but talk to me more about your life," Asked Isaac. "I was traveling with my father when we meet the leaders of the White Cloud. He passed away but wanted me to become more. To live my life fully. Which is what I am trying to do now. What Evelyn has done is unforgivable, she should be put to death for all the damage and death she has caused!" "I agree, I am sorry to hear about your father, and family. I have lost my family too, Sam." "This is why she must pay. I understand why NATO wanted to do this, but it was murder, and then her making us into her little science experiments, it is sick, Isaac". "You are different, Sam! You are a prize! We hope you can teach us how to reverse the effects of this illness. It is in your blood. No matter what they did to create you, it should have still changed your physical appearance, but it didn't, Sam." "I don't know either. I hope I can help, Isaac. Now, that were done with lunch do you think we can go out and search for maladies?" "In a hurry, are you? You won't be! Sam"

   Sam followed Isaac back to the training room. Both were then equipped with one gun, which had some different ammo. It was small, had a metal casing, with a red tip. "What kind of ammo is this Isaac?" "It's poison ammunition, it stuns the malady and then kills them." "This works right? I don't want to be out there with something that does not work, Isaac." "Don't worry about it. You need to learn how to shoot the gun first, Sam." "I know how to shoot, thank you!" Sam lifted the gun and shot the apple out of a dark one's hand. "Max taught me this too! You Jealous yet, Isaac" she asked, laughing. "No, I am not intimidated by him, I can teach you more than he ever could. But I'll give you an A for effort, Sam."

They both were laughing now. Sam was beginning to like someone she thought she never could. Her mind went to Max and wondering what he was doing right now. Sam stopped laughing and asked, "how do you think they are doing? Have you heard anything?" "Chloe has not come back yet. It will be too risky to fly back and forth. She will have to plan her trips. We should get going! We don't want to be out after dark, Sam." Sam and Isaac left HQ and began walking south. The whole area continues to amaze Sam. It looks like she was living on another planet. Most of the buildings where falling, growing vines, trees, and moss. "Why don't you all clean up and start living like humans again?" She asked Isaac. "We aren't humans Sam, we have engineered DNA, that has changed us into a new species. We must create our own life. A new life, Sam." "Where are we going exactly?" Sam asked. "We are going to a malady den, not too far from her Sam." "What is that?" "That is where the maladies live, it is where they feel the safest. They live like a pack of wolves. They search for one another and hide until they get hungry. Then, they search for humans, animals, anything really. Anything which, provides them with meat and blood. The humans who get away, change into either one of us or into a malady. Sam, I thought you would know this."

"Once they are bitten, their DNA changes completely then? Making them seek out one another, for safety and food. That means they are basically re-born. Believe it or not, no one on the White Cloud talks about any of this, not even Evelyn. She either does not know or prefers us to not know, Isaac." "Exactly right, Sam. You must have been good at science. Not many understand the science behind it. It figures that she would not tell you or the crew. If you all are scared of us, then she can control the narrative." "True, Isaac. This means the malady, are injected with a virus. It takes over the body killing healthy cells and reproducing the virus cells, and yes, I am good in science, biology was my favorite subject in school." "It shows Sam, you might be able to show us a few things latter down the road. Now we need to be quiet on the rest of our journey."

Sam and Isaac continued walking silently. They turned north, and Sam could see an old barn. "Look, over there, that is their newest den, Sam" Isaac said in a hushed voice. "They are not that far from the HQ's then. What are we going to do? Isaac" "You will help us destroy them, Sam. We believe you are the one who can help us do that. You have powers that you don't even know you have. Right now, we are going to do nothing, it is time to get back to HQ and continue training," Isaac said. Once Sam and Isaac made it back to HQ, they continued working on

Sam's shifting. He wanted her to visualize fear and engage her panther. After working on it, into the late night, Sam finally did it. She shifted into and out of her panther. "Wow! I did it, Isaac, thank you". "I told you that my methods work. Now tomorrow we work on your other shifts and the power that comes with them. Let's go to bed, Sam". Sam got up and hugged Isaac before leaving to her bunk. She couldn't believe that through all this, she can now change at will into one of her cat forms. On her way back to her bunk, Sam thought about Max and what he could be going through. She hoped that he was doing well and working on the mission. The sooner the mission was over, the quicker she could be with him again. Only if he doesn't die or stay with Jack.

Chapter 14

TRAINING

Before bed, Sam meets up with Rex. "How is your training going, Sam? It has been a long day!" Rex said. "It's been a long day for me too. I was waiting up for you, this way we could catch up," Sam said in a hushed voice. "I did weapons training with them all day. I was teaching them how to be an army unit. I did gather some intel I wanted to share with you, Sam." "We should talk outside, Rex." Sam and Rex walked together to the stairwell. Once inside the stairs, they felt more comfortable to talk. "I found out that some of the dark ones here are not trusted worthy, Sam. Some do not believe that you can help with the malady problem, and we will not win with war with Evelyn. We need to be careful about who we trust. Not everyone wants the war to end." "Well, that is more than I learned today, Rex. You should continue identifying those who are against us. This way, we will be prepared for the battle to come. I learned how to shift in and out of my panther form at will today. I meet the other dark one shifters. They all seem nice, and one may be Max's sister. I have not had time to talk with her, Rex". "That's great, Sam! Congrats! Really? Max's sister! That would be wonderful news for him. You should talk with her when you get a chance," Rex said. "I'll try Rex, but she does not remember much of her past. She changed young, and when that happens, they do not always remember," Sam said. Both said goodnight and headed to their bunks.

The next morning Sam ate breakfast with her new group of friends and introduced Rex to those he hadn't met. "Sam, how is your shifting going," asked Vixen. "I can change into and out of my panther at will." "That is great! Sam" Red said. "How many other cats have you changed into so far?" Asked Jasmine. "I have changed into the panther and the caracal." "I bet you have other farms you can shift into," Maximilian stated. "Yes, that is what Isaac told me. I am not sure, though. We work on that again today, guys" Sam said.

"We all started out with just being able to shift into one other form. It comes in time," Red said. "What about you Rex? What's your story?" Red Asked. "I joined the military young after my family died. I was stationed in Germany during the beginning of the war. I was one of many in the first wave of soldiers who attack the maladies. Many of my friends were killed. Once I realized we were losing the fight me, and a few other men ran. We lived for many months in the mountains until we ran into more maladies. Each day brought more struggles. I was the only one to getaway. That's when I ran into Oscar and moved on the White Cloud. I did not have any other family, it's just my team and me" Rex replied. "That is a lot of death for one man to see. How do you do it" Vixen

Asked? "I just remember what I am fighting for, and the lives of my countrymen, and think, "it's all worth it" Rex explained. Up came Isaac, "it's time to go, guys, we have the training to do."

They all got up, put their dishes away, and said their goodbyes. Sam followed Isaac down to the training room again. "Good morning, Sam, how did you sleep?" "I slept well last night. I was so exhausted. Are we working on bringing out my caracal today, Isaac?" "Yes, that among other things. Go ahead and do exactly what we did yesterday for your panther and apply that to your caracal. What where you feeling the moment you changed? Who was around you? And why you change, Sam."

Sam thought about that day she shifted into her caracal. She needed to have speed and still sneak around in silence. She couldn't think of an emotion. Maybe it was a shift out of necessity. "I don't remember feeling anything, Isaac. We needed speed and agility. I just shifted". "Then think of that now, the need of it, willing the caracal to come out, Sam." Sam closed her eyes, and it did not take long before she successfully shifted. "I did it, Isaac!" "You are beautiful, do you know that? Great job, Sam!" "Yes, you tell me almost daily since I got here. Thanks, Isaac!" "Now change back, smarty pants!" Sam shifted with ease this time. "I think you need to work on shifting while in formation with the army, Sam. We could have Rex come outside with his army and run some drills with us," Isaac stated. Sam agreed, and she and Isaac gathered Rex and the men he was training, to help them.

Isaac lead them outside to an open field, a mile or so

from HQ. It was an old football field. The school was overrun by moss, and part of it looked like a boom dropped right on top of it. The sky was clear, with the sun beaming down on them. All the dark ones looked like porcelain dolls, their skin shined in the sun. Almost like they had rubbed butter all over their skin. Isaac instructed them to start chasing Sam around the track. The closer they got to her, he was hoped it would trigger a shift. Isaac ran alongside her to give her encouragement. Off they went. Sam's heart was pumping, mind forcing her to ask for the caracal, pushing forward, as she ran. She ran so fast that she ended up lapping the dark ones, even Isaac could not keep up with her.

This was not working, she slowed down, to wait for Isaac. As he approached all she could do was a laugh. It was weird to her because she was not even breathing fast, it was nothing for her to run, it was as if she walked. "That's amazing, Sam! You're not even out of breath. Maybe you need to do something else. The caracal cat is light on its feet and silent. You could help Rex train the men, sneaking upon them. Urging the cat to shift." "That sounds like another good idea, thanks to Isaac" Rex said. Sam was starting to like training. Every day it seemed as if she was getting better. Sam and Isaac hung back and allowed Rex and his team to hide out and information. During the training mission, Sam was to attempt to sneak up on and disarm Rex's men. Forcing herself to be quiet, thinking about, and willing her caracal to come out, and it finally did. Sam still wanted to complete the exercise and scare them all. She took one down at a time, till she got to Rex who turned right as she jumped down at him from the ceiling. "Sam that hurt!" Rex yelled. "I got everyone, it worked Rex. Thanks for helping." "Anytime, Sam, where is my team?" "I knocked them out, they should wake up soon." Laughing, Sam and Isaac walked back to HQ.

Sam stayed in her caracal form since she didn't bring extra clothes with her. "I did it, Isaac! Thank you for all your help. You talked about magic or powers the other day. What did you mean?" "A handful of our shifters also have abilities, I guess you can call it magic. For example, Jasmine can become venomous, at will. Maximilian can shoot needles out of his fur, and Vixen can howl at such a high pitch volume, that it ruptures eardrums. These are just a few examples, of course. We think you can do more since you did not change into one of us when you were given the serum. You kept all your human features, Sam." "So how do we find out what else I can do? Isaac." "Time! It did not come to any of the shifters until they learned how to control their shifting. We cannot just guess what you can do. You are faster than any of us, have better hearing and use of your senses without being in your animal form. You may have more in you than even you are aware of," Isaac said. "What do we do until then?" she asked. "We need to keep training, and the more we train, the more you will develop your powers, Sam." "When will we go into combat?" Sam asked. "Not until you have more control over your powers. You can get to know us, and our community until then, Sam." "I will try! Have you heard from Chloe?" "She checked in this morning.

She reported that everything has happened as planned. The people on the White Cloud think you are died along with Rex. They have begun to gather intel on Evelyn and her overseeing agency," Isaac said. "It is official I am dead? I feel alive still (she said with a chuckle), I feel bad for my friends though, Isaac." "I'm sorry, Sam. It will take time! They will forgive you. They will all be excited to see you when they come here," Isaac said.

They both walked into the kitchen, where they found Rex and his men. Sam had no idea how they beat her and Isaac back, but they did. "Do you guys feel brave after losing to a girl!" Sam said. Many of them did not find this very humorous, except for Isaac and Rex. Both were laughing so hard I thought they were going to pee their pants. One of the men named Tre said, "When we rematch you, you won't be the one laughing, we will." "Once I am done training her, she will be better and faster than any of us," Isaac said. Tre just spat and continued eating. Sam and Isaac prepared lunch and sat down together.

"That was funny back there. Have you always been this funny?" Isaac asked. "I think so! Not many find me funny but you and Rex so far". "Well I like it, that is all that matters right now at least, Sam." "Where is Red and the other shifters?" "They are out hunting the maladies right now and for the next few days. They leave for days at a time and come back with many stories of victories," Isaac replied "You're telling me they are out there fighting, and I am stuck here with you all day? What they're doing sounds much more fun then, working with you! No offense, Isaac." "Not funny, by the way. I am helping you become a better shifter, you will become the greatest we have here," Isaac said in an annoyed tone. "I get that, but they are where the action is! Isaac." "It is not always fun, Sam. You know, sometimes we die, or get hurt, we lose friends, and new families are torn apart," he said. "I understand! I'm just anxious about doing something rather than nothing," Sam said in protest. "Since we're done with lunch, we can go for a walk. Walk for your run for me," Isaac said.

Isaac leads Sam outside, and they walk back towards the football field, where they were earlier. Sam spent her walking time exploring the environment. Where each building was, each street name, car positions, exit points, and ways to get back to headquarters. She wanted to be prepared for anything. This could be another training exercise or just a walk. She used her senses to further explore her surroundings. What does it smell like, taste like, and feel like? Isaac broke the silence, "What are you doing? Just now? Sam" "I am taking note of everything around us and how to evade if needed," she said. "You can remember that?" "Yes, ever since I awoke after receiving the serum. I have a heighten senses, they help me map out the surrounding area. It was overwhelming at first, Isaac. I had to learn how to shut it off and focus on one sense at a time. It has been challenging. I can now focus on one or all senses at a time." "You continue to amaze, Sam. This might be an ability of yours," he said. "Where are we heading? We have been walking for a while now," Sam asked. "I wanted to just go for a walk with you. Isn't that okay?" "Yes, I just figured that this was some training exercise, and at any moment someone or something is going to jump out at us." "Not today! Why don't you lead us back to HQ then smarty pants," Isaac stated.

Sam turned them around and began walking them back to HQ. She and Isaac were halfway back when Rex and his team attempted to sneak up on Sam. She stopped walking and motioned to Isaac. Someone was following them. Sam shifted in the blink of an eye into her caracal and walked into the doorway of a building. The building was a single-story, maybe old book store, it was hard to tell. It provided minimal cover from the street. She backed up to the door and hid behind a trash can. She and Isaac were facing the intersection. She had smelled Rex's cologne and was able to identify which direction he was coming from. Sam and Isaac hunkered down, waiting for Rex and his team, to go around past their position. She was not worried about losing this training exercise.

The sun was beginning to set when Rex stepped around the corner. Sam jumped out and was able to disarm all six of them. "Sam your good! How did you know I was coming?" Asked Rex. "Rex, I could smell your cologne!" She said while laughing. "I am not wearing very much! That is crazy! How long have you been waiting?" "We have been waiting for maybe an hour or so, Rex" Isaac said. "With the sun setting, we should go back to HQ," Isaac said.

They all walked back together. Sam loved the view, as the sun was a deep orange, with a pink sunset. Light clouds were beginning to cover the setting sun. She took the sight and the smell of the upcoming rainfall. "It is going to rain tonight," Sam said. "How do you know that?"

Tre asked. "I can smell it coming," she said. "Good job today Sam, you are getting much better at this," Rex said. On their way back to HQ, Sam could see Chloe flying in with a report. She was excited to hear how they were doing on the White Cloud. Chloe met them at the door "Nice to see you all" "How was your flight in, Chloe? What has been happening with Oscar and Max?" Sam asked in an excited tone. "The trip was long! They have traveled many miles since they left. I can't say much more I have to report it to Isaac and the rest of the board before I share it with anyone else". Sam found this odd but brushed it off. "How do you like the ship so far, Chloe?" "I spend most of my time on deck or the loading dock. It is not that much fun or exciting for me, really Sam."

Chloe and Isaac continued walking past the group and into HQ. "Chloe has a message for you sir and mam," Isaac said, trying not to intrude on what they were discussing. "Go ahead and speak Chloe," Robin stated. "Oscar and Max have been doing a great job turning a few crew members to our cause. Evelyn and Jack spoke to them about brining Sam's body back to the ship. Both do not believe Sam has died, but instead that she was taken. Neither wants her to be used against them in future wars. Oscar and Max are doing their best to reject the mission, they are not sure if they will have a choice in the matter. We did find out Evelyn travels from the ship to a base camp in Hawaii. She is gone for three to five days at a time. I followed her to the base camp, but was not able to go inside, due to the safety precautions in place there," Chloe said. "Max and Oscar need to push back against the mission to recover Sam's body. If they are unable to, we will figure out something," Danika said. "Keep following Evelyn to the base camp. Maybe you can identify some of the other members who meet there." Isaac said. Report to them how Sam and Rex are doing in training, and Sam can shift freely between her two cat forms." Isaac stated. "I will do my best, but Evelyn is pushy and smells a rat," Chloe said. "Just keep us posted on how things are going," Jon said.

Sam and Rex walked to the kitchen and waited for Isaac and Chloe to return. Both were excited to hear the news from Oscar and Max. Isaac came into the room with Chloe about 15 minutes later. They reported the news about Sam and how Evelyn is leaving the ship to a camp in Hawaii. Sam was most worried about Evelyn not believing the story that she had died. What could they do to prove this to her? Sam wished that it hopes it does not come down to proof. She and Rex just enjoyed the news and company from Chloe. Shortly after dinner, Chloe left and headed back to the white cloud. Sam decided to shower and go to bed early. She was exhausted from a long day.

After her shower, Isaac was waiting for her. He wanted to take her with him on a recon mission. Sam, of course, jumped at the idea. He would wake her up about four. It really did not matter how tired she was at this point. She would be awake and waiting for him at four. Sam informed Rex, letting him know about the recon mission, and she would not be here when he woke up. He, of course, did not like the idea, but could not go along, he would only slow them down.

Sam and Isaac met in the lobby before going on the recon mission. She and Isaac decided Sam should shift before they arrive at the malady camp. They wanted to be ready for anything. Once Sam had turned, they left HQ. She shifted to her panther form. This would make her invisible in the dark, and not just to the malady, but Isaac as well. It was early morning; the sun was just beginning to rise over the morning fog bank. It had been raining all night, and the ground was very damp and swampy in some areas. The cloud cover was fading, and Sam could tell it was going to be a beautiful day. She and Isaac were half to the maladies camp. Both tiptoed to prevent being seen by any maladies in the area. They climbed up a cliff that overlooked their encampment. The maladies had grown in size, over the last three days. There are over 100 of them gathered together now.

The number of them gathered, amazed Sam and Isaac both. "What's the plan?' Sam asked. "We are doing nothing, just tracking them, and when Red and her team get back tomorrow, we will regroup, and attack." "We came here just to check on numbers, time would have been better spent if Chloe flew over and reported back before heading to the White Cloud" Sam scolded. "That was not my call, I do what I am ordered to, Sam. At least we are not at HQ right now, doing nothing!" Isaac said in a hushed voice.

Chapter 15

MALADIES

At some point, while Sam and Isaac had been sneaking up on the camp, they were spotted. Three maladies had snuck up on them and were waiting for them at the bottom of the cliff. Sam and Isaac looked down the cliff and saw them waiting." "What are we going to do now, Isaac?" Sam asked. "Can you see another way down?" Isaac asked. "I am not sure I might be able to get around them without them noticing. Why don't you start the descent, pretending you have not seen them? While they are looking at you, I will be coming up behind them," she said. "Great plan, Sam, so it begins."

Sam looked down the massive cliff. The way they came up had a trail, it was an easy climb. The other side had sharp crevices, steep decline, with few hands holds. On top of that, there were trees in the way of the decent. Sam shifted back into her human form before starting the descent. She used the trees to help her begin the climb down. The sap from the trees made her hands sticky, but the smell helped cover up the stench of the maladies waiting for them. Once she reached the end of the trees, the cliff had a sheer drop. Sam looked over the cliff and felt fear rising up within her. Can she do this? Sam tied off a rope Isaac had given her to a large tree at the start of the drop. She buckled the carabiner around the harness and began her descent. The rock face had moss hanging down, and it was damp. Sam had a hard time keeping her grip on the stone face. Sam decided to try and repel down as far as she could. That would be better than, slipping and falling the whole way down. With a deep breath, Sam closed her eyes, leaned into the rope and pushed off. With a rush of air, Sam flew off the cliff and hit the rocks below. She winced in pain as she hit, all the way down the left side of her body, she felt pain. Sam still had another 40 feet to go, but the pain in her shoulder was preventing her from holding on the rope with her left hand. She switched from the left side to the right hand and again pushed off the cliff with her feet. This time she kept her feet out, and when she came back to the cliff, she landed on them.

With a smile on her face, Sam pushed off and landed a few more times before she reached the ground. When she unclipped herself, she reached up and rubbed her shoulder. It was bleeding and badly bruised. She had to keep moving, Isaac was counting on her. She undressed and shifted into her panther form. Still, in pain, Sam ran around the cliff and positioned herself behind the maladies. Sam could see Isaac had made it almost all the way down the hill when Sam arrived. She kept in the shadows to ensure she was not observed. He must have been moving slow to save his energy for the fight. Once

Isaac turned around, he could see Sam and motioned for her to attack. At the same time, Isaac and Sam started running towards the maladies. They ran towards him, moving fast. Sam reached them before they reached Isaac. She tore into the first one and had its head off before the others noticed she was even there. The tallest of the three, turned towards Sam, just as Isaac reached them. He attacked the last malady while Sam took out the last one standing. Blood was going everywhere, coming out of the maladies, and spilling on the fern-filled forest. Green turned to red as they finished off the last of the maladies.

Both Sam and Isaac were exhausted and covered in blood. With one look, Sam and Isaac both began the run towards HQ, before the other maladies noticed them and came running. Sam reached HQ before Isaac had. She stopped at the front door and waited for him. "Are you Okay, Isaac?" Sam asked. "Yes, I think so! I don't see any wounds. How about you?" "I think I am fine, just tried and hurt my shoulder when I was coming off the cliff, Isaac." "Let's get inside so I can take a look at it," he said. Sam followed Isaac into the building. She was sore and went into the bathroom to shift before showing Isaac. Isaac, of course, came into the bathroom before she was ready for him. "Really, Isaac! Let me put a towel on". Isaac walked over to her and looked at her shoulder. "That is really bruised Sam, does it hurt?" "Yes, it will hurt more after I shower." Isaac reached in for a hung. Sam could not turn away in time, and when he hugged her, she just broke down crying. "What's going on?" He asked, "I am just hurting, and you have been so nice to me. Thank you, but this walking in on me thing is getting old" she said with a sob. Isaac did not respond. He just stripped down to take a shower while she was getting dressed.

Sam was beginning to get used to a shared shower and bathroom. They just closed the curtain, and everyone does okay. Only Isaac had a hard time following the rules for some reason. When they had finished Isaac helped her get bandaged up, before reporting the fight to his superiors. Sam laid down in her bunk, and just a few minutes later, she was asleep.

Chapter 16

HEALING AND PLANNING

Sam woke up the next morning in horrible pain. She felt like she had been hit by a bus. When she got up there stood Isaac, with a plate of breakfast and a cup of milk. "Good morning, beautiful. Thought I'd make you breakfast today" "Thanks Isaac, it smells wonderful. Let me get up to eat". She tried to sit up for breakfast but cried out in pain. It felt like she broke her arm. "Are you okay?" he asked as he ran to her from the kitchen. "We need a doctor, Isaac! There are none right?". "Nope, sorry Sam, we're hoping someone joining us from your boat will be a doctor." "That will be a long wait. Doc is the only one, I don't think he will come and leave Jack," she said. Isaac helped Sam re-dressed her wound and make a sling for her shoulder. There was not a whole lot Sam could do while she was injured. Her and Isaac sat together and talked about their past and families.

Isaac said, "my family was not the best. I miss them, but my father was abusive. My mother used and allowed him to do all that he did. Now, my grandparents were great. They would take me on the weekends to the beach, swimming, hiking, and many other places. I think I miss the most. I don't know where they are or if they died". "I'm sorry that it is sad. My family was everything to me. None of them were taken by the illness but by other colds and my younger brother fell overboard. I remember everything about them. We did not grow up with much money, but every chance we had, we went hiking, swimming, and did photography. Even my brother, who fought with me every day, I miss," Sam said with sadness in her voice. "That sounds like a great upbringing, is that why Evelyn chose you to experiment on? You are the perfect specimen, Sam" "Why, don't we start planning for our mission. We can plan now, and we will be prepared for the shifters when they get back. Red should be back today, right Isaac?. How many soldiers will we have?" "We have you, and four others. Rex and the 16 soldiers he has been training. Thanks to you, Sam; they will be better!" "23 total, including you! That's not a lot compared to the 100 or more maladies, Isaac." "True, that's why we need a great plan," he said. "Can you replicate the bullets we brought with us from the White Cloud, Isaac? When they fire, they explode on impact. It could take out the maladies faster and save lives. We could even put Rex up on the cliff. He is a great sharpshooter. Then, he can target and blow them up. Do we have any explosives?" Sam asked. "Slow down Sam! We could replicate them, and we might have some left-over explosives from our last mission. The military had it all, but we stole some from a base a while back but were running low?" Isaac replied. "If we can find a way to fire them, we might be able to take out large numbers of maladies without high losses." "Good planning Sam! We have a team member who is great with explosives. I'll set him to the task," Isaac said.

Sam and Isaac continued to plan the fine details. They decided to place Rex on the top of the cliff as the sharpshooter. He could then take out any maladies which were fleeing or sneaking up on the team. Jasmine would stay with Rex and be his back up. Since she could become venomous, all she would need to do is land on the malady attempting to sneak up on Rex, and it would die. Red could also stay with Rex, Isaac suggested since she too was a sharpshooter. Next, Sam, Maximilian, and Vixen would be the first to attack the malady camp from all three sides. One of them could take out many maladies at a time. Isaac and the 16 trained dark ones would attack the rear of the malady camp. They carry the same ammo. The malady camp is held within a large barn. It has two main entrances one at the front of the barn and one at the back. Some of the newest arrivals have just begun to gather outside.

Surrounding the barn was grass fields to the front and hills with thick brush and forest to the back. The barn its self was two-story and had an entry point on the second floor for hay. At the entry point may be a great place to put an explosive. The barn was no longer one color. It had red paint that had begun to fade. You could see the wood beneath the paint, and most of the barn covered in moss. The rear entry had the most advantages for Isaac and his team. It provided the most coverage. Sam and the other shifters would enter the camp already in shift form. The grassland will have provided them with some coverage. A wolf, a bear, and a panther. The maladies may not even realize they are a threat until it is too late.

If they come from different positions, the maladies will not know they are working together. Once the plan had been thought out and drawn up, Isaac presented it to his superiors for approval. Sam and Isaac took the ideas to Rex and the rest of the dark ones. "I think this can work, as long as we get the bullets reproduced and explosives put together. If we do not have either, it will be more difficult to win," Rex said. "We agree! We could be walking into a trap, anything could happen, and there may be additional maladies in the area" Tre stated. "When would we be heading out?" Rex asked. "When Red and the other shifters return from there scouting mission. That should be today, but you never know. The quicker, the better, everyone should be ready to leave as soon as tomorrow night. Rex, you and your team, continue training, and get all the gear ready to go. You and Red will need repelling gear, plus a few extra things for emergencies," Isaac said.

Chapter 17

STEP ONE

Red returned late that night. She and the other shifters were in bad shape. Sam had seen them come in and helped them with dressing wounds, they too would need a few days to heal. Lucky, they heal fast like Sam, cutting their healing time in half. This means they leave for the mission in two days. Red did report unlucky news. She and the shifters ran into a group of ten maladies heading for the same base camp. They attacked and killed all ten of them. All the shifters returned with cuts and bruises. Red had the worst wounds. She had one deep cut to her abdomen, they would need to watch it for infection. Sam spent most of the early morning, cleaning and stitching up the wound. "Hopefully, this heals without getting infected," Sam said. "I agree, it's really sore," Red said in a hushed tone. Within 15 minutes, she was asleep.

As the shifters slept, Sam planned. She knew that by the time the other shifters healed, the maladies numbers would grow tremendously. She wanted them to be ready for anything that came their way. It was not long after Sam fell asleep, that the general alarm in the building started going off. It woke the whole team-up. It was like chaos had struck them awake. Doors and windows began to close, with a metal shutter. "What is happening?' Sam yelled to Isaac! "It must be a malady attack. We all get shut in upstairs with metal doors and shutters. It completely closes us in until the attack is over. This happens from time to time, Sam. They cannot get through the metal. We don't know why, but it works. Let us hope everyone made it upstairs before it closed" He yelled back over the siren.

They all huddled together in the middle of the room, waiting for it to be over. Sam, Vixen, Jasmine, and Maximilian, all shifted into their strongest animals waiting for danger to come. Sam could feel fear from all around her, it was hard to contain. What made it worse is that everyone else was scared or angry. She could hear every scream coming from downstairs over the siren. There were still dark ones caught outside of the shield. It was horrific!

Sam began to shiver, covering her ears, and begging for it to all be over. There must have been many locked out. The screaming continued for a long time. Sam was frozen in time; she could not even bring herself to help those who needed her. Even if she could, there was no way to get to them. Only magic could save them! That was it she thought to herself. What if she could blow up every malady in the building. Dead within a blink of an eye! She had not been given this gift, of extreme senses for no reason. She needed to find a way to use it. Sam began to separate the noise. Taking away the siren, the dark ones who were screaming, and what was left must be the malady.

Nothing was left but a humming sound. The humming came in many different tones. Was this their way of communicating. Each hum was distinct. It sounded like many different bees, all using different tones and occurring all at the same time.

Sam began to think about each tone, targeting each one and sending a pulse from her to them. It felt like Sam had sent out hundreds of lighting bolts at the same time. Striking each malady with the force of an atomic bomb. BOOM! All at once! It scared everyone in the room. The room filled with smoke, and static electricity, little volts sparking between them all, Sam at the center of it. Everyone began to choke and cough from the smoke filling the room. Isaac spotted Sam in the middle of the room, surrounded by her fellow shifters. She was not moving and lying lifeless on the floor. Smoke rolling off her. "Someone gets, me a wet towel," Isaac yelled. Rex ran towards them with wet towels laying them on Sam, hoping it would stop the smoke and sparks from shooting off her. "Is she going to be okay?" Rex asked with sadness in his voice. "She... she... used her abilities to save us, how?" Isaac replied.

The metal doors lifted, and everyone was horrified to see the dead and splattered guts of maladies everywhere. It was gross, like thousands of pounds of hamburger was dropped on them. The smell was even worse. It was like burnt beef. The dark ones who lived, began it funnel into the main living quarters, covered with the remains of maladies. At least 15 had come in from outside, but many of them did not make it. Sam's ability did not save them all, but at least it saved some. She was still unconscious when Isaac picked her up, still covered with wet towels, and placed her in bed.

"She saved them!" Rex said. "I have been telling everyone that she is the key to winning this war and starting our lives over. She used her ability to save us. I don't know how, but it worked. She put out a lot of magic today let her rest. She will be okay," Isaac said. Isaac and the rest of the team began helping those who were saved. Helping them get cleaned up and new clothes on. Isaac radioed the superiors to ensure they were all safe and to tell them what had happened. They had all made it to safety before the lockdown was complete. They ordered Isaac to begin the cleanup and look for other survivors in hiding.

Unfortunately, many dark ones died. Five of the soldiers being trained were killed in the training room. Rex found pieces of them, the maladies tear into anyone they find. This made Rex even angrier, he had begun to make friends and here go the maladies killing them again. Cleanup would take time and a strong stomach. The whole building really stunk. There was burnt flesh seared to the walls and floors. Bones shattered, sticking out of walls and everything had been painted with red blood. Rex had never seen anything like this before. Even during the many years of war, he was in throughout his military career.

Days had passed since the maladies attacked HQ. Most of the remains had been removed, from the walls, floors, and ceiling. They were all still stained with the blood of the maladies and dark ones alike. Isaac had continued planning' they're attacked to the malady camp. The superiors were pushing for revenge. This was the most significant lost yet, and the dark ones could not outlast the maladies if they did not start to fight back. Ian, Danika, Robin, and Jon were all in agreement, "We need to strike back now. We cannot keep waiting for Sam to wake up. It has been five days since the BBQ. We need to proceed with or without her, Isaac." Jon stated with elevated voice and tone. "We need to just wake her and get on with the attacked. You and Sam had this planned out days ago, just make it work without her if need be," Robin said. "The shifters will not do it without Sam. No one in Rex's team will move forward either. Rex has been training replacements for the five we lost, and they will be ready by the end of the week. I sent out a recon mission yesterday, who reported that the maladies were still gathering at the barn location. Just give me until the end of the week. I beg you! We need her," Isaac said. "Sunday, with or without her you leave, understood?" Danika ordered. "Understood" he replayed. "Before you go, we received news from Chloe. She reported that the White cloud is not giving up on Sam. Max and Oscar recruited ten people who are willing to leave the ship and help us here. They arrive by Sunday. Max will stay behind and continue to report messages back to Chloe. He has made the decision to stay behind and state that he had no idea what Oscar was planning, and he was the reason Sam died. Hoping this will stop Evelyn from looking for Sam," Jon reported. "I'll get quarters ready for ten more than and hope Sam wakes up. Is that all," He asked. "Dismissed," they said in unison. Isaac rejoined Rex and gave him the news. He was excited to be seeing his friends again but worried that Sam was not going to be ready to fight by Sunday.

Sam had horrifying dreams. She heard men and women dying, humming of the maladies and then an explosion. It was like a recorder that continued to repeat over and over. She could hear the calls of her friends and others willing her to wake. Isaac kept talking to her, but she could not move or speak to him. She could not even open her eyes. This did not make sense to her. What happened? Isaac had told her about everyone being overjoyed she had saved them. Sam did not remember saving anyone. He even told her of his affections, that he would do anything to see her beautiful eyes again. Isaac did not expect to like her in this way. Throughout the training, he found himself becoming more and more drawn to her.

This was all confusing to her! Where was she? She wanted nothing more than to wake up and speak to them all. What was happening in her mind? She could not stay asleep forever; they need me! This was not what she wanted, she wanted to save people not to hear them die. Sam had lost all sense of time during her sleep. She did not know what day it was or how long she had been in this state. Sam was in the middle of a dream when an unfamiliar voice screamed her name. "Who is there? I am stuck, someone, please help me!" Sam asked. "You must help yourself first! No one can help you out of this. You used magic that no one has been able to unlock since this experiment started. You can change everything," the voice said. "How can I get out of this endless sleep?" She asked. "Will it, just like you did when you saved the lives of those stuck outside with the maladies." She heard nothing more from the strange voice, she yelled, asking for help but nothing. She thought about what the voice said. That she could awake, she needs to just will it so. Her mind was telling her something, what was it... She went back into the dream or was it a memory, she did not know. She remembers hearing the screaming, sirens, and humming, that humming. It was maladies! What did she do, "Think, Sam, think!" She told herself. Right then, Sam opened her eyes! I killed them all with... my magic? Isaac ran to her side, "you're awake!" He reached down and pulled her head in for a kiss. It was powerful, it pulled her into him. Caressing his face and hair, Sam forgot everything, and just kissed him. At that moment nothing else mattered. Not Max, or the war happening around her, only Isaac and Sam.

Chapter 18

THE AFTERMATH

Sam opened her eyes to Isaac, sleeping beside her. She was in the main housing room, and it was early. The sun had not risen and began to light up the kitchen. She pulled herself away from Isaac and found herself in the kitchen. She was hungry, felt like she had not eaten in days. How long was she asleep? She made herself a tasty breakfast and enjoyed it while watching the sun come up. It was a beautiful morning sunrise. The sun was bright orange with rays of pinks, reds, and yellow peering over the mountains in the distance. Sam could almost feel at home, sitting in front of the big bay window at her house. As she was enjoying her food, Isaac joined her. He gave her a gentle kiss and sat beside her. "You scared me, Sam! I was not sure you were going to wake up". "I was scared of myself. I almost didn't wake up. I just kept having a recurring dream, about the maladies and what happened. I heard you talking to me and many others telling me their stories and thanking me. Then, a voice I don't know drew me out of it. Told me that I am the only one that has opened my magic since the experiment started, all I needed to do was will myself awake," she said. "That is very odd, Sam. A male or female voice?" "Male, older, maybe and I did not recognize it from anywhere, Isaac." "That needs further exploration, but right now we need to get ready for battle, it starts tomorrow at dawn. Sam, you need to bring that magic of yours with you if you were going to win this war". Sam just smiled and finished eating with Isaac.

They were interrupted shortly after by Rex. "May I have a word, Sam?" "Of course, always Rex." They walked out into the stairwell, where they always talked outside prying ears. "What are you doing? You're with Isaac now? What about Max? He is on the White Cloud alone. I hope you know what you are doing Sam!" Rex scolded like any father would. "Rex, I don't need a dad right now. I feel something greater with Isaac, I can't explain it, but it is happening. I am sorry for Max, but I am a different person now. He cannot understand who I am, nor would I expect him too. I am different, I may not be able to have children or carry a normal life. I am not going to ask him to wait for me, in the hopes that we will both be the same person. I hope you understand and can accept my decision. I was told about Max's decision and the ten who will be arriving here tomorrow. I hope one of them is doc. We can use his help. Are you ready for this fight, Rex? You will have Red and Jasmine helping you." "I am ready, but are you? It has only been a day since you woke up," Rex asked.

"I know Rex, but I can do this. I can hear the maladies. They talk in a humming noise, using different tones back and forth. I can lock into them and destroy them. I know I can, Rex. Trust me!". "That is amazing, Sam but be careful, you are a weapon! Now both sides will want you, and I am worried that you will be stuck in a battle between two sides of the same coin. Max will be on one of those sides and Isaac on the other. Yes, I am fathering you but only because I care, Sam". "Noted Rex and I am no body's weapon!".

The mission needs to be on Sam's mind, not Max and Isaac fighting over her. She had chosen Isaac! That is what she is sticking with, at least that is what she was telling herself. Sam spent her afternoon with everyone really. Just enjoying their company, not knowing if any of them would be coming home with her. Or her coming back to them.

Chapter 19

THE BATTLE BEGINS

Sam and Isaac woke up at three the morning, day of the mission. She and the rest of the shifters prepared for battle. Each shifting into their strongest animals. Sam into her panther, Jasmine into the horned dung beetle, Vixen into a Serbian Husky, Maximilian as a Kodak bear. All of them were the strongest and most substantial of their species. Jasmine can pull 150 lbs more than her body weight. She was a beautiful red and black beetle. She scurried about waiting to leave. Vixen chose the husky because it could withstand the longest run over varied terrain. She was an orange and gray husky, with white intermixed both colors. Maximilian was a Kodiak, the largest of all bears in the world. He would tower over every man. He was dark brown with black throughout his body. Red never shared with Sam or anyone, what or who she shifted into. She preferred to stay in her dark form. Isaac might be the only one who knew what she turned into.

Everyone stood around, staring at the four of us. Isaac

reached out and rubbed my ear. "I see everyone is ready! You all have your orders". Sam, Vixen, and Maximilian will take the front of the barn, spread apart and will attack first. Rex, Red, and Jasmine will take the highest cliff and begin shooting those they can, and Isaac with the 16 of who were trained by Rex will take the back of the barn. The trees will protect them for some time, but eventually, they will be noticed. "We are to stop any retreats through the back of the barn. Everyone has new ammo that will explode on impact. If anyone has any doubt now, I'd the time to voice them." Isaac stated. No one objected. They made their way to the lobby and split up. Isaac kissed Sam before he left, "Stay safe and remember to use your abilities! We will all make it home safe". "Isaac, thank you for everything if I don't get the chance to repeat it." One last kiss and he was gone. Sam, Vixen, and Maximilian left the lobby and headed South toward the open fields, they each planned to stay together until they were a mile out from the barn. The grounds were dead quiet, no sounds, the wind was not even blowing. Sam had a feeling they were walking into something they were not prepared for. She could smell the wheatgrass surrounding them, it was ready to be harvested. Except, there was no one here to collect them anymore. The sun was still down, and the chill was still in the air. Sam could see the stars in the distance. The sky was open for miles, no clouds to be seen. She and the shifters did not talk to one another, not even a whisper until it was time to split up. "Good luck, guys! I will see you when the fight is done," Sam said.

Both Vixen and Maximilian just nodded their heads and

walked away. Sam paused her position, taking in everything she could see, hear, and taste. Sam needed to clear her mind and focus on finding everything that hummed. She began to walk towards the barn, crawling through the wheat field, waiting to pounce like an ordinary house cat, seeking prey. Every move was slow and positioned just right towards her target. When she was about seven to ten yards away from the front of the barn, Sam could hear the humming of each malady around the barn. She did not remember how to lock on to more than that at a time. Sam sat and awaited the signal to attack from Rex and Red. She and the others sat for what seemed to be an hour or more. Then, a loud, echoing shot rang out. It was so loud that it, startled Sam, and she had to refocus. All at once, Sam and the next bullet hit its target. Sam blew up twenty or more maladies, they exploded with light, and smoke. More gunshots rang out from the cliff. The battle had begun! Humming maladies caught off guard began to turn and run towards the shifters. Maximillian roared and shot out thick poisoned needles, into the oncoming maladies. Vixen sent out a high-pitched scream that ruptured the ears of each attacking malady. At the same time, Rex and Red searched for targets from above. The shooting followed by the explosion of maladies heads. Isaac and his team began shooting shortly after as maladies tried to escape from the rear of the barn.

It was like time its self had stopped. Blood, lighting, gunfire all happening in concession, with one another. Jasmine had begun to target maladies that were coming up the cliff to attack Rex and Red. Sam took a breath, paused her connect to look around at the damage. Maximilian was struggling to keep the maladies at bay, Vixen was hurt and running towards Sam for help, Isaac was getting overrun, and he has lost eight men. Sam could not lose him or anyone else she cared for. She breathed in and focused on the humming everyone she could find. Red and Rex noticed her pause and begun to shoot those after her. One after another, they began to protect her. She only needed a minute to take in power and disburse it into all the maladies in the camp.

Sam exploded with power, sending lighting into the bodies of all the maladies which were communicating with each other. Explosions were happening all around her, from Red and Rex's gunfire, Isaac and his teams firing at the retreating maladies. When Sam was finished, she had cleared out 75% of the attacking maladies, Vixen and Maximillian were able to break free and continue to fight those who were left. They ran towards the open barn. Sam watched as Vixen was run down by retreating maladies. There was nothing Sam could do. The look on her face was that of relief, as she fell to the ground. Sam heard her last heartbeat leave her body. Sam was perplexed, she did not understand what she saw, Vixen was glad to be dying, that couldn't be right! Sam turned her attention to what was in front of her. She tore into each malady she ran into. They tasted like death. Sam did not want to not swallow the blood or body parts torn from the maladies. As they made their way into the center of the barn, Sam could see many humans remains along with dead dark ones. The smell of rotting flesh overwhelmed her nose.

Some of those who had been bitten had begun the turning process.

Sam could hear their strange hearts beating. She and Maximilian had cleared the rest of the barn when Isaac and his six remaining dark ones entered the room. "Yuck! The smell is overwhelming," Tre said. "Yes, it is! Where is Vixen?" Isaac asked. "She did not make it. She is back there." Maximillian said. "Did you get them all?" Sam asked. "No! Maybe 10-15 got away". Tre responded. "We won this fight, but it came at a high cost. How many of the humans are alive Sam, can you tell?"

"Yes, it seems that five have begun the changing process. It is hard to tell if they will be dark ones or maladies yet." "Sounds good, we need to gather our dead and wait for the change to be complete. We will have Red and Rex stay posted, and Jasmine can come down here to help us." Isaac called to them over the radio to report what he wanted them to do. He gave them their orders, and Jasmine made her way to the barn. "Sam, please stay here and keep an eye on the changing humans, while we start to gather our dead men and woman." Isaac reached out and caressed Sam's head as he walked by. She was glad he was not hurt and the same for herself.

Sam observed the carnage before her. There were body parts thrown about, blood, and guts everywhere. Flys had begun to gather and have a feast. Sam could hear the buzzing of their wings, flying from one malady remain to another. The sun had even come out. The temperature had begun to rise, and Sam could feel the warmth in her bones. It had been a long, cold, and exhausting night.

Sam struggled to stay awake, she used up most of her energy in the fight.

The humans would change soon; it would only take a few short moments. Theses had to of been freshly caught. Moments later, Sam heard small voices coming from all five bodies, prepared for anything Sam called out for Isaac. "They are awake!" When the first one stood up, Sam was in complete shock, it was a young girl maybe 12. "Don't be scared we won't hurt you?" Isaac said. "I am April, where am I?" She was about 80 pounds of nothing, and her whole life has now changed. Brown hair and green eyes. She seemed sad and lost. "Just come on down all of you, we will explain what we can," Isaac said. The second dark one was an older man, 6-foot-tall, stocky, with black hair and eyes. He said his name was Scott. Next, came an older woman five foot nothing, with black hair and red eyes. She told us her name was Lauren. The fourth one awake was another young woman, maybe 16, with orange hair, and blue eyes. She said her name was Ginger, and the last to awake was a young man who said he was April's brother. His name was Mike.

Since all five were confused, scared, and covered with bites and blood, Isaac decided to talk with them outside and away from a large talking panther and horror scene happening in the barn. He explained to them what had happened and what they have now turned into. He explained to them what shifters are and powers one may have. They were tired of the change, and Isaac had one of his men walk them to HQ. There they could get cleaned up and eat. Sam went outside to help with the gathering of the dead. Her heart sunk, as she took in all the death, this was all because Evelyn wanted to experiment on the human species. There is too much blood on her hands. She deserves to die! But Sam knew that killing her would not end what she started. They needed to do more, find out more, and do their best to stay alive. Sam would never guess what is coming next.

I hope you have enjoyed reading my first book. I will be writing more books for this amazing series. My focus is to engage our young readers and encourage them to read more and surf the web less. This book was written to and for young readers, with no sexual content or foul language. Book 2, The Dark Ones will be coming out by the end of this year. Please visit my web page, and Face book page for updates and videos.